CLAIMING THE CITY IN SOUTH AFRICAN LITERATURE

This book demonstrates the insights that literature brings to transdisciplinary urban studies, and particularly to the study of cities of the South. Starting from the claim staked by mining capital in the late nineteenth century and its production of extractive and segregated cities, it surveys over a century of writing in search of counterclaims through which the literature reimagines the city as a place of assembly and attachment. Focusing on how the South African city has been designed to funnel gold into the global economy and to service an enclaved minority, the study looks to the literary city to advance a contrary emphasis on community, conviviality and care. An accessible and informative introduction to literature of the South African city at significant historical junctures, this book will also be of great interest to scholars and students in urban studies and Global South studies.

Meg Samuelson is Associate Professor in English and Creative Writing at the University of Adelaide, Australia, and Associate Professor Extraordinaire at Stellenbosch University, South Africa. She has published widely in South African, African, Global South and oceanic literary and cultural studies.

TRANSDISCIPLINARY SOUTHS

Russell West-Pavlov (Universität Tübingen, Germany)
Molly Brown (University of Pretoria, South Africa)
Guadalupe Valencia García (Universidad Nacional
Autónoma de México, Mexico City, Mexico)
Philip Mead (University of Melbourne, Australia)
Dilip Menon (University of the Witwatersrand,
Johannesburg, South Africa)
Sudesh Mishra (University of the South Pacific, Suva, Fiji)
Sunita Reddy (Jawaharlal Nehru University, New
Delhi, India)
Fernando Resende (Universidade Federal Fluminense,
Niterói/Rio de Janeiro, Brazil)
Jing Zhao (Xi'an Jiaotong-Liverpool University,
Suzhou, China)

How might we theorize, think, articulate and critically/creatively inhabit the multiple and overlapping Souths of today's world? How do we enable these Souths to speak to each other, question each other, in ways that complement and expand the work upon which they are already embarked with each other? It is becoming increasingly clear that in order to better understand and contribute to the multiple processes and ways of becoming-Souths, a radically transdisciplinary approach to the study and analysis of, critical interventions in, and dialogues within and between Souths needs to be implemented. Intersectional thinking at the crossroads of race and ethnicity, class and labour, gender and corporeality, not to mention climate change and ecological destruction, demands a combination of perspectives and methodologies to deal adequately with complex planetary dilemmas. This series offers a hospitable forum for innovative intellectual inquiry that seeks to break out of extant disciplinary frameworks so as to address new questions emerging from contemporary Souths. Facilitating cross-border exchanges and polyglot negotiations between the most disparate fields of intellectual and scientific inquiry, thereby resisting the disciplining effect of enclave-thinking, the series aims to contribute to the transformation of knowledge production and associated practices across multiple Souths.

As a gesture of international solidarity, the editors of the series TRANSDISCIPLINARY SOUTHS donate the editors' royalties to the charitable organization PRO ASYL e.V. in Frankfurt am Main. PRO ASYL supports the cause of asylum seekers by providing public advocacy and legal advice.

HOSPITALITIES
Transitions and Transgressions, North and South
Edited by Merle A. Williams

EAST AND SOUTH
Mapping Other Europes
Lucy Gasser

CLAIMING THE CITY IN SOUTH AFRICAN LITERATURE
Meg Samuelson

For more information about this series, please visit: https://www.routledge.com/Transdisciplinary-Souths/book-series/TRDS

CLAIMING THE CITY IN SOUTH AFRICAN LITERATURE

Meg Samuelson

Routledge
Taylor & Francis Group

LONDON AND NEW YORK

First published 2021
by Routledge
2 Park Square, Milton Park, Abingdon, Oxon OX14 4RN

and by Routledge
605 Third Avenue, New York, NY 10158

Routledge is an imprint of the Taylor & Francis Group, an informa business

© 2021 Meg Samuelson

British Library Cataloguing-in-Publication Data
A catalogue record for this book is available from the British Library

Library of Congress Cataloging-in-Publication Data
Names: Samuelson, Meg, author.
Title: Claiming the city in South African literature / Meg Samuelson.
Description: Abingon, Oxon ; New York, NY : Routledge, 2022. |
Includes bibliographical references and index. |
Identifiers: LCCN 2021016080 (print) | LCCN 2021016081 (ebook) |
ISBN 9780367763930 (hardback) | ISBN 9781032004389 (paperback) |
ISBN 9781003174189 (ebook)
Subjects: LCSH: South African literature (English)--History and criticism. |
South African literature--History and criticism. | Cities and towns in literature.
Classification: LCC PR9355.5.C57 S26 2022 (print) | LCC PR9355.5.C57
(ebook) | DDC 820.9/35868009732--dc23
LC record available at https://lccn.loc.gov/2021016080
LC ebook record available at https://lccn.loc.gov/2021016081

ISBN: 978-0-367-76393-0 (hbk)
ISBN: 978-1-032-00438-9 (pbk)
ISBN: 978-1-003-17418-9 (ebk)

DOI: 10.4324/9781003174189

Typeset in Times New Roman
by Deanta Global Publishing Services, Chennai, India

CONTENTS

ACKNOWLEDGEMENTS

This little book is based on an extensive survey over a number of years during which I incurred more debts than can be acknowledged here. Among the many who sustained it, I wish to name those who helped assemble convivial and stimulating environments in which to read, think and write in the English Department and African Doctoral Academy of Stellenbosch University and the Department of English and Creative Writing at the University of Adelaide, including Nwabisa Bangeni, Brian Castro, John Coetzee, Dawid de Villiers, Dorothy Driver, Annie Gagiano, Rob Gaylard, Ralph Goodman, Louise Green, Rachel Hennessy, Matt Hooton, Ashraf Jamal, Jill Jones, Nick Jose, Dirk Klopper, Ben Madden, Achille Mbembe, Stephen Muecke, Julian Murphet, Grace Musila, Sarah Nuttall, Ros Prosser, Daniel Roux, Lynda Spencer, Tina Steiner, Maggie Tonkin, Mandy Treagus and Shaun Viljoen.

At the University of Cape Town, I benefitted from conversations and collaborations with Philip Aghoghovwia, the late Harry Garuba, Khwezi Mkhize, Christopher Ouma, the late Constantin Sofianos, Hedley Twidle and Sandy Young; and, at a time of crisis, I found a welcome intellectual home in the New Generation Professoriate led by Robert Morrell – the more engulfing global crisis of 2020–2021 afforded me the happy opportunity to reconnect with members of this collective via online meetings of the Southern Theory Reading Group.

Another notable group is the 'Shifting Cities' collective: although we did not progress beyond the second round of our bid, workshops in Dakar and Johannesburg with Olutayo Adesina, Harry Garuba, Kizito Muchemwa, Robert Muponde, Tom Odhiambo, Remi Raji, Godwin Siundu and Flora Veit-Wild laid guiding beacons at an early stage in this research.

I have been blessed with the opportunity to supervise an extraordinary cohort of postgraduate candidates and postdoctoral fellows; those whose studies have directly or tangentially informed this particular project include Olujide Adebayo-Begun, Esthie Hugo, Doseline Kiguru, Kizito Muchemwa, Kudzayi Ngara, Kathleen Samson and Lynda Spencer.

Practical assistance was provided by a number of librarians on three continents, among whom I wish to single out the staff of the African Studies Library and Interlibrary Loans at the University of Cape Town. Christine Emmett and Esthie Hugo provided stellar research assistance and the Faculty of Arts and School of Humanities at the University of Adelaide offered necessary support in the form of teaching relief and research leave. Nadia Davids, Peter McDonald and Uhuru Phalafala helped me to locate copyright holders. I appreciatively thank Mongane Serote and Jeremy Cronin for permission to quote from the poems *No Baby Must Weep* and 'This City'. Every effort has been made to track the copyright holders of 'Golden City Blues' sung by Dolly Rathebe in *African Jim*; I apologise for any omission in this regard and would welcome notification on how to obtain permission for quotation thereof.

I am pleased also to acknowledge the professional and prompt editorial and production support offered by the team at Routledge, particularly Aakash Chakrabarty and Anvitaa Bajaj, and the 'Transnational Souths' series editor, Russell West-Pavlov, who responded to my proposal with characteristic efficiency and enthusiasm.

To the many others who created or contributed to forums in which this study was developed or who have otherwise hosted and fed the ideas presented in it: my grateful thanks.

I dedicate this work to Dorothy Driver, who has been a teacher, mentor, colleague and friend to me over a period of twenty-five years, and who offered guidance and support throughout the writing of this book.

1

INTRODUCTION

[H]ere we are all still prospectors, with a digger's claim on
the earth beneath our feet ...
— Ivan Vladislavić, *Portrait with Keys* (2006a)

The city has claimed much attention in South African literature. From the
first urban settlements to contemporary conurbations, writers and perform-
ers of the national literature have been invested in the constitution of the
city, returning repeatedly to address the claims that have been staked on
it while issuing ones of their own. This book surveys these claims across
more than a century, from the origins of the industrial city and through the
colonial-apartheid period (hyphenated to emphasise continuity) to the first
two decades of the democratic state.[1]

The first towns within the borders of present-day South Africa began
to develop after the Dutch East India Company established a victualling
station at the Cape in the mid-seventeenth century (the precolonial city-
state of Mapungubwe had been abandoned by the early thirteenth century),
and primarily served the maritime trade as ports and centres of agriculture.
This orientation was maintained under the British occupation until the second half of the nineteenth century when a new and distinct form of cityness began to take shape around the 'digger's claim' in the colonial mining
towns of Kimberley and Johannesburg (Vladislavić 2006: 60). The model
initially hammered out on these claims would be reproduced in segregated
cities that were even more rigidly divided after the apartheid regime came
into power in 1948 and then again, albeit differently, under the neoliberal
conditions of the global order that South Africa entered after it emerged
from its exceptional state.

Parsing Johannesburg in the early twenty-first century, Vladislavić
(2006: 18) shows that it continues to be shaped by the geological structure of its mineral deposits and the industry of their excavation; as he
walks its streets, the narrator finds that '[a] spine of rock, an outcrop of

the gold-bearing reef on which the city depends, blocks every thorough-fare between the avenues'. Constellated in this image is the way in which the fragmented surface of the city, as well as the regulated flows of traffic across it, arise from the condition of being 'undermined' (Vladislavić in Knecht 2005).[2] It is this city, and those that come to be fashioned after it, with which this book is concerned – a city that is, in short, characterised by the combined procedures of extraction and enclaving. Attentive to the ways in which the literature contests its exploitations and exclusions, while treasuring the freedoms or attachments that it promises, the study tracks the mutating forms of this city from the early mining camps to the near present.

The discovery of diamonds and then gold, in 1867 and 1886 respectively, set South Africa on a dramatically different course. Previously little more than a strategic seaport en route to Britain's imperial 'jewel', it now attracted expansionist ambitions in its own right. Cecil John Rhodes, who secured a monopoly over the diamond diggings through his company De Beers Consolidated Mines, dreamt of drawing a 'red line' through the continent with a 'Cape to Cairo' railway while devising schemes to annex African land and corral black labour. After gold was found in the Boer Republic of the Transvaal, the struggles over land and labour that the availability of diamonds had fomented intensified further.[3] Within a few short decades, the second South African (or Anglo-Boer) War (1899–1902) had been fought and won by the British, the Union of South Africa had been declared (1910), and the African majority had been dispossessed by the Natives Land Act of 1913, which assigned most of the country to white ownership, apportioning a mere 7% (later increased to 13%) for African reserves. Sol Plaatje (1998 [1916]) recognised that the latter condemned the native to one of two pos-sible fates: 'to slave for farmers or descend into the bowels of the earth to delve the gold which enslaves the world'.

Already in 1891, Olive Schreiner had observed that 'the great Johannesburg gold-mines' had 'drawn men from all parts of the earth' (Schreiner 1923: 46),[4] with Africans, she estimated, accounting for nearly 90% of the population (the actual proportion was less, though still well over half). By the end of the decade, the 'instant city' (Matshikiza 2008) that sprung up amidst the diggings is described by her in terms redolent of the definition that Georg Simmel will give to the metropolis as 'the seat of the money economy' (Simmel 2004 [1903]: 13): 'On first walking the streets', writes Schreiner (2005 [1899]: 74), 'one has a strange sense of having left South Africa, and being merely in some cosmopolitan centre, which might be anywhere where all nations and colours gather round the yellow king'. Yet the rule of the 'yellow king' is surely felt more keenly than elsewhere in Johannesburg, which was by this time producing up to a quarter of the gold in circulation (Berger 2009: 69). It will come to impose distinctive structures on this city, and on South African cities more generally, while bonding them to the global economy.

Both commodity and currency, gold is primarily valued 'as the guarantor of the capitalist world's monetary system' (Ross 2008: 72). When first unearthed in the Transvaal, it had already displaced silver to become 'the foundation of the global economic system' and 'its primary means of exchange' (Mbembe 2008: 40). Founded on its underground gold reserves, Johannesburg has always been integrally connected to the capitalist world system, its apparently unique forms having been designed for the purpose of extracting bullion and funnelling it into a globalising economy. The constitutive claims staked by mining capital sought to maintain tightly controlled flows of labour into compounds in order to better exploit both the peoples and resources of the region, while ensuring a racial monopoly over the wealth that the city would generate. Much of southern Africa was pushed and pulled into migrant labour through an intricate system of taxes, influx control regulations and pass laws. Housed in compounds, barracks and hostels, and later in ring-fenced townships, those who toiled underground to produce the city's wealth were determinedly denied their own claims on the city.

The tension between traffic and enclosure that might be said to animate all cities is thus heightened in South Africa, where various claims on the city are asserted and refused through the struggle to regulate or release movement into and through urban space. It persists in the apartheid period with its raft of legislation aimed at fixing different categories of persons in place while availing the white population of the benefits of black labour, and it is reorganised again in the post-apartheid city's hyperbolic manifestations of the enclaved constructions that are the paradoxical urban face of neoliberal deregulation. Traced across this history, a tension between traffic and enclosure can be seen to drive and direct the 'dialectic between the underground, the surface and the edges' that Achille Mbembe and Sarah Nuttall (2008: 17) have identified as 'the main characteristic of the African modern of which Johannesburg is the epitome, and perhaps even of the late modern metropolis itself'. Homing in on its figures – from train and mineshaft to walking and driving in the city, and from compound to fenced township and gated community – this book considers how they have been appropriated and enlisted in the clamour for the 'right to the city' (Lefebvre 1996).

Henri Lefebvre's advocation of 'the right to the city' has particular pertinence in South Africa, in which urban centres were constructed to serve an extractive economy and designed according to an ideology of 'separateness' that sought to deny citizenship to the majority. Perhaps recognising that the 'right of the citizen' is invested in cities, and that '[t]o exclude the *urban* from groups, classes, individuals, is also to exclude them from civilization, if not from society itself' (Lefebvre 1996: 195), the apartheid state extended and strengthened the restrictions through which mining capital enlarged its profits. 'What gave apartheid its particularly cruel twist', notes Mahmood Mamdani (1996: 29), 'was its attempt artificially to deurbanize a growing urban African population'. Those who were not endorsed out of the city altogether were removed from inner-city neighbourhoods, rehoused on the outskirts in segregated townships and permitted to return to the centre only in servile roles and on the most temporary terms. In articulating the 'right to the city', Lefebvre notably refers to the prerogative to access or be accommodated in the city, and to inhabit the centre rather than being edged into peripheral ghettoes. This translates also into a claim on the city as 'a spatial-temporal unity' and of 'gathering together instead of fragmentation' (Lefebvre 1996: 195). A substantial part of the 'demand and cry' for 'urban life' is, moreover, the right to co-author the city and its functions (Lefebvre 1996: 158). A city, Lefebvre (1996: 117, 65) argues, might best be conceived and experienced as 'the *oeuvre* of its citizens' – a collective and constantly re-made work of art which contests the 'tendency towards money and commerce, towards exchange and *products*' that seeks to impose its structures on the metropolis. Literature is one domain in which this right is repeatedly claimed, and perhaps even realised.

The diachronic approach of *Claiming the City* reveals the evolving and recursive nature of the literary claim as it is iterated across the century, as well as how cityness, or the quality of being urban, is represented at various historical junctures in the national story. While tracking the forms of the South African city through time, the study is also interested in its place in the world and seeks to identify the ways in which this urban experience is both distinctive and illustrative. As such, it follows interventions that foreground the distinguishing features of cityness in the 'postcolony' and the global south, as well as those that approach southern cities as exemplary or revealing of processes beyond themselves.[5] There is growing recognition that what passes as 'urban theory' is largely based on the experiences of northern cities. Ananya Roy has thus called for 'new geographies of theory'. Her intervention is, importantly, 'not an argument about the inapplicability of the EuroAmerican ideas to the cities of the global south'; what she submits instead is that, '[a]s the parochial experience of EuroAmerican cities has been found to be a useful theoretical model for *all* cities, so perhaps the distinctive experiences of the cities of the global South can generate productive and provocative theoretical frameworks for *all* cities' (Roy 2009: 820).

This position is akin to what Jean and John Comaroff call 'theory from the South'. While the 'Global South' has been a moniker for the 'developing' world, they propose thinking of it rather as being 'ahead of the curve' of world-historical processes, as well as where 'the effects of those processes tend to most graphically manifest themselves' (Comaroff & Comaroff 2012: 16, 13). Because 'most colonies were zones of occupation geared towards imperial extraction', the postcolony prefigures 'the rise of neoliberalism' in particularly stark ways, and the South remains the 'frontier' of its 'unfolding history' (Comaroff & Comaroff 2012: 15, 38). Viewed in this light, we might read South African cities not as sites of exception, even though they are in many respects remarkable, but rather as 'staging grounds' and 'laboratories' (Comaroff & Comaroff 2012: 5) for global apartheid and for the combined exploitation and laying waste of certain categories of being, as well as of the earth itself. 'Theory from the South' is not simply diagnostic of global and planetary processes, however. It also recognises the African postcolony as 'a source of inventive responses to the contingencies of our times' (Comaroff & Comaroff 2012: 18), precisely because it has felt the sharp edge of the knife.

In this spirit, *Claiming the City* attends to the particular forms and experiences of the urban in South Africa while at the same time locating their distinguishing features within global procedures of advancing inequality and precarity. It claims literature, also, as a medium through which the 'most compelling insights into the lived dynamics of everyday life in African cities come to us', to quote Edgar Pieterse (2011: 10), Director of the African Centre for Cities in Cape Town. These insights, notes Pieterse, show up the paucity of the 'developmental' model that continues to be applied to cities of the South and offer a wealth of alternative paradigms and positions. Not least, as this book seeks to show, South African literature has through its various claims on the city archived and composed practices of sustaining life, nurturing community and dignifying death that – in the face of the extractive and enclaved economies consuming and dividing ever more of the world – might be deemed both priceless and essential.

Notes

1 The study focuses on South African literatures written in English while including selected landmark texts in translation from other languages. In so doing, it recognises that the national literary tradition is largely, though by no means entirely, written in English (see Mphahlele 1983: 31).

2 As Vladislavić elaborates: '[t]he deepest mines in the world are on the Witwatersrand, they're now mining at nearly four kilometres under the surface. And that idea, the idea of Johannesburg as a city that is 'undermined', is a very powerful metaphor that's been used by several writers, the sense that we're on the surface and underneath' (in Knecht 2005: np).

3 On the impact that the discovery of its mineral wealth had on South African history, and on the management of land and labour in the early mining towns, see inter alia Meredith (2007), Ross (2008: 59–121) and Berger (2009: Ch. 4).

4 Appearing first in the *Cape Times* in 1891, the essay was republished posthumously in *Thoughts on South Africa* (1923).

5 I take up Mbembe's notion of the 'postcolony', which identifies 'a given historical trajectory – that of societies recently emerging from the experience of colonization and the violence which the colonial relationship, *par excellence*, involves', and evoke his understanding that 'the postcolony is a particularly revealing (and rather dramatic) stage on which are played out the wider problems of subjection and its corollary, discipline' (Mbembe 1992: 3).

2

ALL THAT GLITTERS

> Johannesburg had always been depicted as a city of dreams,
> a place where one could transform oneself from a poor peas-
> ant to a wealthy sophisticate, a city of danger and opportu-
> nity ... It was eGoli, the city of gold, where I would soon be
> making my home.
>
> – Nelson Mandela, *Long Walk to Freedom* (1994)

Nelson Mandela's recollection of the attraction that the city exerted on a young man from the countryside resonates with those one might find elsewhere in the world. Yet the Johannesburg in which he arrived in 1941 presented a particular set of opportunities and dangers stemming from its position as the 'city of gold' in a racialised capitalist state. Approaching it in the evening, the young Mandela is enthralled by the 'maze of lights' seen 'glinting in the distance': '[i]t all seemed tremendously glamorous' (Mandela 1994a: 51). On reporting for work as a night watchman at Crown Mines, however, he quickly learns that '[t]here is nothing magical about a gold mine' (Mandela 1994a: 55). Nonetheless, the city maintains an ambiv-alent attraction. Life in the township of Alexandra, where he makes his first home, is said to be both 'exhilarating and precarious' (Mandela 1994a: 66). One aspect displays its deprivation, another declares that '[i]ts atmos-phere was alive, its spirit adventurous, its people resourceful'; 'hellish' in its poverty, it is 'also a kind of heaven' as one of the few areas in which Africans could own freehold property 'and become permanent city dwell-ers' (Mandela 1994a: 66–67). Alexandra thus promises a different claim to that presided over by the mine, with its segregated hostels and townships that are little more than 'prisonlike compound[s]' (Mandela 1994a: 56, 59). But though this 'Dark City' falls beyond the pale of the enticing 'landscape of electricity', it is by no means exempt from state surveillance and control; on the contrary, it is subject to 'regular' police raids in which 'masses of people' are 'routinely arrested ... for pass violations, possession of liquor,

DOI: 10.4324/9781003174189-2

and failure to pay the poll tax' (Mandela 1994a: 51, 66). Even here, then, the 'city of dreams' appears elusive.[1]

The forms of cityness that were being concretised in Johannesburg by the time of Mandela's arrival were rehearsed in the diamond fields of Kimberley. Attracting fortune-seekers from around the globe after 1867, it quickly grew into the second-largest settlement in southern Africa (Ross 2008: 59). By 1881, it housed the first Stock Exchange on the continent and, in the following year, became the second city in the world to install a municipal infrastructure of electric street lighting ('Kimberley' 2020). Olive Schreiner sketched an early portrait of the proto-city in the narrative fragment 'Diamond Fields', which she penned circa 1873 in what was then still called 'New Rush'. The mine is shown animating the scene 'like a huge heart'; around it forms a social world characterised by 'the whirl and rush and tumult of many thousand wheels and voices', the 'din of machinery and babel of tongues' (Schreiner 1974 [1873]: 14, 13). This 'babel' appears expressive of the invigorating clamour of the city as a place of 'convergence' (Lefebvre 1996: 195), but it is orchestrated in service to the 'money economy' (Simmel 2004 [1903]: 13) under extractive colonial conditions – and race and capital will soon be used to assert an exclusive claim on it.

White diggers successfully lobbied the Cape government to deny black claims and Rhodes's De Beers Consolidated Mines in turn 'swallowed up all competing interests' to establish its monopoly, capitalised by a new system of migrant labour in which profits were maximised by confining workers in closed barracks (Berger 2009: 68–69). Two defining features of the South African city were thus inaugurated: 'the racial bifurcation of the industrial labour force and the housing of black migrant labourers in compounds' (Ross 2008: 63).[2] From here on, Africans would have no claim on the wealth that they extracted, nor on the urban life that it financed. A further innovation to arise from the diamond diggings was the extension of the railway-and-port network, which for the first time achieved the 'mercantile integration' of the region (Ross 2008: 64), ferrying tens of thousands of workers to the compounds, and siphoning off what remains to this day the largest stream of diamonds in circulation.

When the 'tumult' that Schreiner observed around the 'big hole' of Kimberley moved to Johannesburg after 1886, it carried with it this new infrastructure of mobility and containment. The racialised labour practices forged upon them were further elaborated in response to the nature of ore deposits on the Witwatersrand Reef.[3] Although vast quantities of gold are lodged in the reef that extends beneath Johannesburg, the deposits are uneven and of low concentration. The reef was thus mined at deeper and deeper levels, with a corresponding rise in both cost and danger (the Witwatersrand today still boasts the deepest mines in the world, with Mponeng now nearing a depth of 4km). The punishing and exorbitant process of extraction again led to the rapid consolidation of small claims into mining houses, which accrued major economic and political muscle that they proceeded to flex across the region. Unlike diamonds, however, the price of gold was fixed to an international standard; cartels and even monopolies could not drive it up. Instead, profits were increased by tightening the squeeze on labour. With the support of the colonial state, mining companies sought to access and control ever larger reservoirs of labour in order to keep salaries at a minimum in what are sometimes described as being among the more dangerous and exploitative working conditions on earth. Denying Africans the 'right to the city' was critical to the claim of the mining houses.

Glittering with the allure of a place in which 'one could transform one-self from a poor peasant to a wealthy sophisticate' (Mandela 1995a: 51), the city of gold was constructed in such a way as to secure its goods for the exclusive use of a white minority. The steady stream of labour required to access these goods was achieved by casting a dragnet in the form of a bevy of taxes across the countryside, and those who continued to hold fast to the soil were soon shaken loose by the Natives Land Act. To render their labour more exploitable, much-despised pass laws imposed precarity on those who, like the young Mandela, sought to make home in Johannesburg. Yet, for all its dangers and disappointments, the city remained 'a magnet for Africans from the countryside' (Mandela 1994a: 59).

'Oh, I came to Joburg ...'

Oh, I came to Joburg, the Golden City
Oh, what did I come here for?
– Dolly Rathebe, 'Golden City Blues' (1949)

'All roads lead to Johannesburg', declares Alan Paton's *Cry, the Beloved Country* (1948); '[t]hrough the long nights the trains pass to Johannesburg' (Paton 2000 [1948]: 12), having stretched across the country and reached deep into the continent.[4] The mass migration thus conveyed to the industrial city is a dominant theme in the literature – one often called 'Jim comes to Jo'burg' after the feature film *African Jim*, also known as *Jim Comes to Jo'burg* (1949). Lewis Nkosi is perhaps the first to identify it, as well as to observe the ideological baggage that it carries:

Most vernacular novels, as well as those written in English, ... worked and reworked the theme of 'Jim Comes to Joburg', in which it was implied that Jim's loss of place in the tightly woven

9

tribal structure and the corresponding attenuation of the elders' authority over him was the main cause rather than the result of the nation's tragedy.

(Nkosi 2016 [1965]: 17)

The feature from which the theme takes its name is rather atypical in that it concludes with the successful urbanisation of its protagonist. *African Jim* might even be said to mesh urban and rural through the performance by Dolly Rathebe of 'Golden City Blues', which she had improvised to the tune of 'Salt Lake City Blues' in the audition that won her the role of Africa's first film star, and which notably replaces the wholly urban orientation of the original with a yearning reference to the 'kraal' (see Samuelson 2008; Dovey and Impey 2010). It does, however, contain elements of the theme that attracted the scorn of Nkosi and other members of the *Drum* set (to whom we turn in the next section). These include poking fun at the rural naïf as he encounters urban sophistication or presenting a cautionary tale in which those who lack the sense to flee from it are shown to be consumed by the city. Veering between tragic and parodic modes, the theme tends to emphasise the incongruence of the urban African. Various written and performance works reprise or reject it in what might be seen as the first round in the literary struggle to claim the city.

Stephen Gray locates the inaugural novelistic appearance of the 'Jim comes to Joburg' theme in *Leaven: A Black and White Story* (1908) by the South African-based English journalist Douglas Blackburn.[5] *Leaven* presents the great drama of urbanisation, while tracing the continuity from diamonds to gold, through the adventures of Bulalie who, emerging exuberantly into modern subjectivity, is enchanted by all that is 'novel' (Blackburn 1991 [1908]: 25). Little having changed in its reception since Gray identified it as the 'great and neglected' (Gray 1985: 63) contribution to this theme, its plot is rehearsed here in some detail.

Bulalie is first introduced in a rural setting in which space is expansive and time organic: he gazes upon 'the long wide valley below him' as the sun sets behind 'the blue hills many miles away' (Blackburn 1991 [1908]: 1). Far from a pastoral idyll, however, the scene that he scans is one in which he waits for the police to appear and across which a rival has returned from the mines bearing desirable goods, including a concertina. Bulalie resolves to leave so that he, too, may return carrying 'wonderful' things that that would make him 'great in the kraal'. At this point, an extradiegetic narrator intervenes to place his individual story in politico-economic context: 'Thus without knowledge Bulalie justified the political economists of Natal who preached the gospel of forcing the native to work by fostering a desire for the luxuries and trivialities of civilisation'. The story shows these luxuries to be a corrupting force bringing conflict to the village when Bulalie's father castigates him for his desires while himself drunk on urban liquor. Defending himself against the assegai that his father would wield against him, Bulalie inadvertently commits parricide. The pull of city things is now matched by the push of the law, and he sets off toward the 'glittering lights' of the town of Pietermaritzburg and, ultimately, the golden city.

Bulalie's passage from peasant to proletarian takes place via an infrastructure of road and railway and through various roles. First, he joins a road-making party, where he learns from a canny companion about the mines of Kimberley and Johannesburg, as well as of the need to dissemble in the colonial economy (his companion's strategy is to pretend that he is 'fresh from the kraal' and knows nothing of the techniques he has mastered), and who passes an illegal rough diamond to Bulalie when arrested for stock theft. Bulalie proceeds to take work as a domestic servant in Pietermaritzburg (a role he finds unsatisfying) and sojourns at a mission-station (equally tiresome) before selling his labour to a mine-contractor in the 'blackbirding' trade who smuggles his 'lot' across the Natal border and delivers them to the Witwatersrand.

In contrast to both the kraal and the mission, the mine compound, which brings together Africans 'with speech and customs so different to his own', offers excitement and a 'bustling gaiety' that is matched only by the city streets, where Bulalie thrills at the spectacle of 'men and women as plentiful as mealie stalks in a big garden' (Blackburn 1991 [1908]: 130, 131). The extradiegetic narrator intervenes again to comment on Bulalie's 'delight … with the new life': 'He neither knew nor cared to know that the conditions amid which he lived [on the compound] were unique, abnormal; that they represented only the sordid, brutal side of the white man's civilisation' (Blackburn 1991 [1908]: 131). While assuring readers that 'Bulalie was not a fool', the narrator directs his story towards the recognition that escapes him. His narrative thus takes a tragic turn: the compound becomes his grave when he tries to save a do-gooder missionary from a conspiracy hatched by the mine manager and liquor traffickers. Through this redirection, Blackburn critiques also the divisions imposed by the compound structure between the groups in whose mingling Bulalie had previously delighted.

As signalled in its title, the register on which Bulalie's story concludes is both unequivocal and sustained in RRR Dhlomo's novella, *An African Tragedy* (1928). The first book of fiction published in English by a black South African,[6] *An African Tragedy* was produced by the Lovedale Mission Press, a provenance that evidently exerted an influence on the attitudes displayed therein. Whereas *Leaven* critiques colonial capitalism, and what later readers would recognise as the prototype of apartheid's procedures of engendering 'separate development', while mocking evangelical amelioration efforts, Dhlomo's narrative visits Johannesburg only to retreat from it in dismay and disgust. Showing the city to have a corrupting influence on its hero, Robert Zulu, the novella also construes it as a source of contagion that threatens the integrity of rural life when he returns to infect his wife and their unborn child with syphilis.[7] The concluding resolution displays a decisive turn away from urban, seeding hope for the future in a quarantined countryside.

In contrast to Dhlomo's wholly dystopic figuration of the city are the more ambivalent responses that labour migrants expressed through adapted or newly activated performance genres. For instance, the *sefela sa setsamaea-naha le separloa-thota* ('songs of the inveterate travellers') that were produced and performed by Basotho migrants en route to the mines recast their experiences through trenchant rural images and forms. An idiomatic constant is the 'cannibal' ('*lelimo*') (Coplan 1985). Ethnomusicologist David Coplan teases out the complex encoding of the city in this trope: it is a metaphor for 'the earth itself, which consumes the miner in its belly', as well as for the 'boss boys' and white miners 'who push black workers to the point of exhaustion in their gluttony for power and higher pay', and the contractors or 'bloodsuckers' (such as Blackburn's 'blackbirder') who similarly extract profit from their labour, but it refers also to the faction fights in which Basotho *marashea* (or 'Russian') gangsters 'both defended and terrorized Basotho communities in South Africa's urban locations' (Coplan 1994: 7). An ambivalently multivocal sign, then, 'cannibal' simultaneously signifies oppression and agency, destruction and defence.

Equally ambiguous is the train, which is another recurring figure in this genre. Conveying labour from the countryside to the mines, and later from the black townships to the white city, trains describe the lines that exclude Africans from making a claim on the city by reducing their presence therein to a transitory servicing role. Extracting labour, trains are, moreover, the medium through which the countryside is underdeveloped and African sovereignty undercut. The train thus often functions as an emblem of black exclusion from urban modernity as well as 'of the *destructiveness* of white industrial power' (Wade 1994: 87). At the same time, for the peasant-proletarians who shuttled between the two, the railway was sometimes perceived more positively as forging 'a tangible link between rural and urban life, hitching together the dissonant worlds of the country and the city' (Comaroff & Comaroff 1987: 191).

This 'hitching together' is replicated in orature that draws the train into the idiom and rhythm of indigenous poetics. For instance, in 'Praises of the Train', delivered in Sesotho by Dimitri Segooa in 1941,[8] it is seen to crawl across the countryside like a 'black centipede' (Segooa 1982 [1941] 62). Thus introduced in familiar terms, the locomotive is reproved as the 'all-devourer ... that carries to the mines a man's village' (Segooa 1982 [1941]: 62, 63). The rupture that it introduces reorganises relations of space and time: defeating the cyclical temporality of the countryside ('I vanquished the sun ... and the jet black night'), the train races across space, 'outmatch[ing] the horse' as it 'rush[es] on, fixed to time' (Segooa 1982 [1941]: 62, 63). Coming 'from where no one knows', it cuts through the lands of the 'sacred spirits'. And yet, as the medium to earning the taxes levied by the colonial state, it is simultaneously the vehicle that 'defend[s] the villages from captivity' (Segooa 1982 [1941]: 62).[9]

Nguni-speakers also adapted the oral *izibongo* (or 'praise poetry') genre to manage their entry into the colonial economy. In a performance recorded in Zulu in 1948, Nja-Mlungu Majola describes 'riding the mail train to the land of the mine dumps!' and ironically modifies the royal greeting to address his new employers: 'Bayethe, bayethe, you Boers!' (Majola 2002 [1948]: 130). *Isicathamiya*, the acapella choral music of Zulu migrants, similarly works to connect 'heterogenous worlds' (Erlmann 1991: 158); for instance, the song '*Shosholoza*' ('go forward') recounts the journeys of Ndebele migrant workers transported over vast distances in a 'fast moving train'.[10]

Though understood to advance a coercive cash economy and the exploitation of labour, the connective infrastructure of the railways is not received as coherently oppressive; nor is it seen to be unidirectional. Goods, stories and songs travel back and forth along its tracks, as do migrants who straddle the division between country and city. The urban monetary economy is moreover shown to reorganise rather than terminate rural relationships: Blackburn's Bulalie, for instance, resolves to seek work in the city in order to become 'great in the kraal' (1902: 2) by securing cash with which to procure cattle on his return to the countryside. Absorbing these perspectives, the colonial city is characterised by the presence of competing, rather than coherent, discourses. Schreiner, as we have seen, alludes to the 'babel' issuing from the big hole that organises the labour relations which will come to shape all South African cities, while *Leaven* reproduces the jostle of contending discourses and socio-dialects in heteroglossic prose (see Gray 1991; Bakhtin 1981 [1975]). Like other cities, these are sites of 'encounter', 'gathering' and 'convergence' (Lefebvre 1996: 129, 195); even within the constraints of its colonial manifestation, the act of rendering the urban experience brings forth new voices, registers and genres from the mélange.

This is exemplified in the Xhosa-language poetry of Nontsizi Mgqwetho, published in the Crown Mines newspaper *Umteteli wa Bantu* during the 1920s. Mgqwetho appropriates the mode and diction of the *izibongo* while adapting it to the print medium. Urbanisation is shown to damage African self-determination and to rent the social fabric; at the same time, it enables the emergence of the woman poet. The poet who 'rouses the court' and 'censure's the king' is, she notes, 'always male' (Mgqwetho 2007 [1920]: 3). It is, paradoxically, only in the city that the critical license of praise poetry, which was traditionally performed by men, becomes available to her as a medium through which to critique urban mores: it is 'here in this land of thugs and booze' that 'these female poets' are 'first encountered' (Mgqwetho 2007 [1920]: 3). Mgqwetho thus celebrates and emulates Charlotte Manye Maxeke,[11] who led a successful campaign against attempts to extend pass laws to women in 1913: 'Go and we'll follow you', she proclaims to the 'woman who protested passes' (Mgqwetho 2007 [1920]: 4).

Such emergent forms articulate city and countryside in an unstable binary between which the diegetic thread of the 'Jim comes to Joburg' morality tale can be seen to unravel. This instability is both product and expression of the 'fraudulent and inherently contradictory' nature of colonial modernity (Attwell 2005: 4), in which 'the institutions of modern life' were introduced by a state that simultaneously 'depriv[ed] people of the rights that were associated with the project of modernity itself' (Gikandi 2003: 337). Recognition of this duplicity is evident in Mgqwetho's refrain: 'Reds and Christians need passes to travel'. The complaint is that Africans who abandoned traditional ways at the colonial behest are subject to the same restrictions of movement as those who spurned the introduced practices associated with western modernity (the moniker 'Reds' refers to the ochre-stained blankets worn by Xhosas who refused to convert). In his later memoir, Peter Abrahams (1954: 260) puts it thus: 'the peasant', having 'found the tribal economy inadequate when the new taxes, the new offerings and new prices of the white men came', is 'turned into a townsman, a modern man who was part and parcel of the highly industrialised world of the present', only to then discover that the 'good things' of the city are "RESERVED FOR EUROPEANS ONLY"'.

HIE Dhlomo – younger brother of the author of *An African Tragedy* and a shining light in the modern vanguard dubbed the 'New Africans' (see Couzens 1985; Masilela 2007) – responds to the imposed documents that restrict African claims on the city in the play, *The Pass* (1943). His poetic masterpiece, *Valley of a Thousand Hills* (1941), presents in turn the rapacious reach of industrial urbanisation into rural settings: the city is shown to extend its maw across the land and the dichotomy that would preserve the countryside as a pastoral haven is again destabilised. Another 'New African', BW Vilakazi, writing in Zulu, joins Mgqwetho and Dhlomo in observing the degradation of the countryside and the evisceration of African autonomy by the industrial 'money economy' radiating outwards from the city. The first African to be appointed to the academic staff of the University of the Witwatersrand, where he was conferred with a doctorate for a thesis on 'Oral and Written Literature in Nguni' (1946), Vilakazi is seen to have mediated his own sense of alienation in the white city through the figure of the migrant labourer (Zondi 2011: 174). The poem '*Woza Nonjinjikazi!*' ('Come, Monster of Steel') (1945) apostrophises the train as a 'steely monster' that has 'swallowed' him along with 'many others' (Vilakazi 1973 [1945]: 20). If, however, the poem adopts the idiom of the 'inveterate travellers', the nostalgic glance back at the countryside is that of the alienated urbanite: longing to retreat from the 'bustling crowds' that the train encapsulates, the speaker wishes that he 'could hide' himself '[a]t home among the mealie-stalks' (Vilakazi 1973 [1945]: 21).

In *Ezinkomponi* ('The Gold Mines'; lit. 'On the Mine Compounds') (1945), Vilakazi juxtaposes the labouring black body and the machine that exacts its sweat and blood. Initially, the machine elicits empathy as one 'no less enslaved', and as expendable, as the bodies of black labour: both have been delivered by train to the mines in order to manufacture wealth for others; and both will be discarded and left to die with 'damaged lungs and ebbing strength' (Vilakzai 1973 [1945]: 124) once they have been exhausted. But the poem proceeds to drive a wedge between miner and machine, indicting the latter for drowning out the worker's 'cries and groans of pain' and inferring the relationship to be one in which 'you are the masters – we the slaves!' (Vilakzai 1973 [1945]: 126). The tone is first appeal, then warning. '[W]e too may have no pity', it predicts, when that future day arrives on which a triumphant cry will address these 'things of iron': 'You are the slaves of black men now!' (Vilakzai 1973 [1945]: 127).

Though in conclusion turning again from the industrial city toward an ancestral embrace, Vilakazi here anticipates a future irrevocably bound to the machine and acknowledges that the rural retreat is no longer available to him: the 'mealie-stalks' among which he sought reprieve in the previous poem are now found to be 'shrivelled' while the huts that they nourished stand 'empty' (Vilakzai 1973 [1945]: 126–127). It is, after all, precisely because the land has been 'plundered' by 'foreigners' that the speaker's 'black brothers' have flocked to the mines (Vilakzai 1973 [1945]: 128; as Paton's novel puts it, before repressing this recognition to advance a pastoral vision, '[t]he soil cannot keep them anymore' (Paton 2000 [1948]: 8). Even when located as antithetical to the city, then, the countryside is shown to have been deformed by the urban rather than imagined as a pristine land apart from it.

Vilakazi's poetry is also prescient of Raymond Williams's observation that the city produces 'critically altered relationships between men and things' (Williams 1975: 201), as well as of the more recent recognition that 'the city is everywhere and in everything' and that it functions as a 'machinic assemblage' (Amin and Thrift 2002: 1, 5). Abrahams – whose childhood and youth in the urban slums and the surrounding countryside is recorded in his autobiographical *Tell Freedom* (1954) – registers this also in *Mine Boy* (1946), which has been billed as 'the first modern novel of black South Africa'.[12]

Depicting Johannesburg as an assemblage fabricated for the extraction of gold, *Mine Boy* presents the enveloping 'din' that rises from all quarters, harmonising to sound out the very essence of the city:

> The rumble of trams and trains, the noise of cars, the voices of people, the tramp of feet, all these created a din that was at once divorced from its causes and had an individuality all its own.
>
> A clear, distinctive hum, throbbing from the bowels of the earth, from the mouths and hearts of men, from the machines, and rising. Rising high above its causes.
>
> (Abrahams 1963 [1946]: 84)

This 'hum' is orchestrated at the particular conjunction of space and time that composes cityness. Simmel notes that cities must operate according to 'the strictest punctuality' if they are to coordinate their disparate parts and practices, and to 'integrate' the 'relations and activities' of the 'differentiated interests' that populate it, into the 'highly complex organism' that is the metropolis (Simmel 2004 [1903]: 14). Presenting urbanisation as entry into such a conjunction, Abrahams's novel opens with the rural character, Xuma, disoriented on the streets of Johannesburg while a clock chimes 'One ... Two ... Three' (Abrahams 1963 [1946]: 1). Initially bewildered, Xuma comes to master the city by establishing a novel identity as proletarian proto-citizen, as one who leads the nightshift and sets the city's throbbing pulse.

First, Xuma must come to terms with the 'strange' new reality of the mine, which is defined by two alarming observations: the pacified masculinity that he reads in the eyes of the compound miners, which reminds him of 'sheep that did not know where to run when the dog barked'; and, the sudden descent of a cage into the earth that, in leaving behind a 'vacant hole', paradoxically reveals the operations of colonial capitalism, or what the novel describes as the 'seeing of nothing for a man's work' (Abrahams 1963 [1946]: 41, 39, 42). The efforts of the men who labour underground are, moreover, iteratively effaced on the surface:

> A truck would come from the heart of the earth. A truck would go up to build the mine-dump. Another would come. Another would go ... And for all their sweating and hard breathing and for all the

redness of their eyes and the emptiness of their stare there would
be nothing to show.

(Abrahams 1963 [1946]: 42)

Yet, whereas Xuma finds himself barred from restaurants and forced off
the pavements of the city, the mineshaft transports him to an experience
of manhood that cuts across race. Though awkward when they meet on the
streets, Xuma, the 'boss boy', and 'his white man', the gang leader Paddy
(called the 'Red One' by virtue of his hair colour but also in anticipation of
class solidarity), 'worked shoulder to shoulder' underground; deep in the
bowels of the earth, they are simply '[t]wo strong men. A white man and a
black' (Abrahams 1963 [1946]: 106).

If, however, the mine offers a potential platform for the performance
of proletarian prowess, it simultaneously threatens to sap the strength of
working men. Xuma learns of 'the sickness of the lungs and how it ate a
man's body away' when he sees a miner coughing blood, while 'gold dust
streamed upwards to make [other] men wealthy and powerful' (Abrahams
1963 [1946]: 107–108). The narrative crisis follows the detection of an
underground water leak that is declared safe by the mine engineer, but
which renders the chasm a grave for those who work it. When Xuma and
Paddy's counterparts on the dayshift are trapped by the collapse of rot-
ted scaffolding, Xuma is emboldened to initiate a strike. The novel would
have readers receive this as proletarian protest – as the realisation of what
it calls the 'beautiful dream' of non-racial class struggle. Xuma, it is said,
'felt stronger than he had ever felt in all his life. Strong enough to be a man
without colour', and, when the mine manager calls the non-strikers to one
side, 'Paddy walked over to Xuma and took his hand' (Abrahams 1963
[1946]: 181).

Although Xuma, unlike Paddy, manages to escape the police who arrive
to break the strike, the novel ends with him surrendering in solidarity with
his white fellow worker. In contrast to the sacrificial conclusion of *Leaven*,
this positive proletarian identification – including as it does Xuma's refusal
of the assigned role of disposable labour that is figured in the devouring
mine – lays an unambiguous claim on the city. Xuma's journey from the
countryside may have been motivated by his family's loss of cattle (like
Bulalie, he intends to make his fortune and return home), but by the time
his story concludes his consciousness is emphatically urbanised; unlike
Bulalie, he does not require a narrative *deus ex machina* to avert an ending
that would reinstate the rural as the proper place of the African subject.

Imagining a new society founded on the solidarity of labour, rather than
one determined by race, orients Xuma toward the city in ways unavail-
able to writers under the formalised apartheid instituted after the National

Party's electoral victory in 1948. Also stillborn are the liberal ideals professed in *Cry, the Beloved Country* mere months before the elections. Like *Mine Boy*, Paton's novel concludes with a black man taking a white man's hand; conversely, however, the proposed antidote to racialisation is a return to rural feudalism rather than urban proletarianisation.

Echoing the portrayal of *An African Tragedy*, Paton's novel focalises the city through the eyes of the Reverend Stephen Kumalo of the mission station in Ixopo. It is a perspective that receives the city through a lens of moral disgust and social dismay. Conveyed by train from pastoral hills that are said to be 'lovely beyond any singing' (Paton 2000 [1948]: 7), he finds himself hurtling through an industrial landscape that is 'too much to understand' (Paton 2000 [1948]: 18) and in which both Zulu customs and the Christian practices of the rural mission stations are shown to have disintegrated into debauchery. Kumalo travels to Johannesburg in search of his sick sister and missing son – that they are respectively found to be a prostitute and a murderer is indicative of the city's corrupting influence.

Whereas the novel seeks to align the reader's perspective with that of the astounded and appalled reverend, its rendering of the urban heteroglossia that Kumalo experiences as confusing cacophony allows unauthorised voices to erupt into the narrative. His brother, John Kumalo, issues one such voice, and becomes a fleeting spokesperson for urbanisation before the narrative dismisses him as a charlatan. Claiming that the city has released him from systems of rural patronage that bind Africans to colonial capitalism, John cracks open the contradiction at the heart of the novel's pastoral dream – namely, that its vision of African 'emancipation' (Paton 2000 [1948]: 236) advances a state that casts them as subjects rather than citizens.[13] At variance with the nostalgic timbre and rural orientation of the dominant narrative voice, John proclaims: '[i]t is here in Johannesburg that the new society is being built' (Paton 2000 [1948]: 34). Identifying with this position are the writers associated with *Drum* magazine, who established themselves in explicit opposition to *Cry, the Beloved Country* and its unwitting endorsement of the incoming apartheid regime's designs – drawn more sharply than before – to restrict African horizons to a rural existence punctuated by urban servitude.[14]

The 'fabulous decade' of *Drum* magazine

It was the best of times, it was the worst of times; it was
the age of wisdom, it was the age of foolishness; it was the
season of hope, it was the winter of despair …
– Can Themba, 'Crepuscule' (1972)

The 'fabulous decade', claims Nkosi (2016 [1965]: 20), 'spelled out the end of one kind of South Africa and foreshadowed the beginning of another'. *Drum* magazine was its 'barometer' (Chapman 2001 [1989]: 185) and Sophiatown, the inner-city freehold suburb from which Stephen Kumalo sought to rescue his sister, its highly mythologised setting.[15] Founded in 1951 as *African Drum*, the magazine initially projected a rural sensibility, constructing the city as a place of dreadful delight that sensible characters shun. This message was expressed through its serialisation of *Cry, the Beloved Country*, as well as its debut short story, Alfred Mbaba's 'Rhodesia Road' (1951): both cherish the stability of rural life and associate the city with avarice and moral degeneration. The magazine was, however, soon set on a different course. A much-cited comment presents the guiding position elicited from a reader survey:

> Ag, why do you dish out that stuff, man? Tribal music! Tribal history! Chiefs! We don't care about chiefs! Give us jazz and film stars, man! We want Duke Ellington, Satchmo and hot dames! Yes, brother, anything American. You can cut out this junk about kraals and folk-tales and Basutos in blankets – forget it! You're just trying to keep us backward, that's what! Tell us what happening right here, on the Reef!
>
> (qtd. in Sampson, 2005 [1956]: 20)

Whereas much prior and subsequent black writing looks back to the countryside or restages the drama of urbanisation, the magazine that was henceforth rebranded as *Drum* orients itself almost entirely towards the urban present while attracting onto its staff a group of writers who would forge notably new directions in black fiction and journalism. This turn was both literary and political: it rejected Paton's pastoral aesthetic along with apartheid policies that claimed the city as the preserve of white citizens. As Can Themba (1985 [1961]: 115) puts it: 'the authorities decided that the whole process of African urbanization should be repudiated ... And the simple method projected was the retribalization of the people'. The counterclaim that he and other writers associated with *Drum* made on the city was asserted in the face of this brutal scheme.

Nkosi, who cut his writing teeth on the publication, enthuses of *Drum*: 'It wasn't so much a magazine as it was a symbol of the new African cut adrift from the tribal reserve – urbanised, eager, fast-talking and brash' (2016 [1965]: 22). Though dominated by advertisements and advice columns promoting consumer culture among a recently urbanised population,[16] the magazine played a significant role in encouraging and accommodating black writing. Some of its writers, such as Nkosi and fiction editor Es'kia

Mphahlele, also went on to become pioneering cultural critics, and later described the style developed in *Drum* as 'urbane, ironic, morally tough and detached' as well as 'agitated and impressionist' (2016 [1965]: 24; Mphahlele 1992). The energies and constraints of the city determine literary form. 'It is not so much the intense suffering (though this helped a great deal) which made it impossible for black writers to produce long and complex works of literary genius', Nkosi (2016 [1965]: 30) observed of the period, 'as it is the very absorbing, violent and immediate nature of experience which impinges upon individual life'. What Nadine Gordimer (1976 [1968]: 180) describes as the 'fragmented and restless form' of the short story was the preferred mode for expressing the vertiginous individuality of urban existence as well as its precarity under apartheid, while non-fiction written 'in a storytelling style that prefigured American New Journalism' (Driver 2012: 395) bore witness to the ways in which the city impressed itself upon its residents, and boldly announced the urban I/eye. Linguistic play, code-switching and generic experimentalism in turn articulated the 'swarming, cacophonous, strutting, brawling, vibrating' life of Sophiatown (Themba 1972 [1959]: 104) in defiance of the state programme of 'separate development' that was pursued through the forced removal of urbanites from this cosmopolitan centre into compound-styled townships on the outskirts of Johannesburg or 'endorsement' to rural reserves that were now called 'Bantustans' or 'Homelands'.[17]

While many have debated whether the 'glamour and cheesecake' of *Drum* was mere escapism or a form of camouflage (Matshikiza 2001: x), its glitzy sensationalism might be seen to perform a politics of aspiration and refusal that in itself issued a compelling claim on the city. Gordimer, who fictionalised *Drum's* milieu in her second novel, *A World of Strangers* (1958), notes of the pervasive jazz culture that 'the music and the dancing were not a dream and an escape, but an assertion' (Gordimer 1962 [1958]: 128). In *Drum* itself, this declaration is communicated in a range of registers from anecdote, romance and thriller to 'serious chronicles of the urban struggle for survival' (Rabkin 1975).

Exemplifying the latter are Es'kia Mphahlele's 'Lesane' (1956–1957) stories, which are set not in Sophiatown but in the neighbouring Newclare. The story cycle presents black urban life bracing itself for assault on a street personified into 'rows of dilapidated houses that stood cheek-by-jowl as if to support one another in the event of disaster' (Mphahlele 2001 [1956b]: 133). In contrast to much other writing in *Drum*, these stories are set on 'the quietest street' (Mphahlele 2001 [1965a]) and rendered in sober realism and standard English. The emphasis is on documenting what Mphahlele (1983: 28) later called 'the drama of survival', and on demonstrating how 'communal life' (Gaylard 2004: 275) is reconfigured rather than disbanded in the city. The urban melting pot is celebrated, but so too are the customs that have been carried over from the countryside, and much attention falls on the intricate negotiations through which the disparate peoples assembled on this street come to comprise a new community. Rooted in everyday urban life while nourished by customary practices adapted from the villages of their forebears, theirs is an assuredly unselfconscious claim on the city:

> Outside there in the street the young folk were dancing. Dancing as if yesterday they didn't have a riotous beer-spilling raid; as if tomorrow they might now have a pass and tax raid ... And in all this there was a spirit of permanence which they felt, without thinking about it.
>
> (Mphahlele 2001 [1956b]: 134)

On the other end of the stylistic spectrum are Arthur Maimane, Casey Motsisi and Themba, who perhaps most epitomises the *Drum* ethos. After his early death in exile following his banning in South Africa, Nkosi (1972: xi) eulogised of him that 'to have known Themba ... is to have known a mind both vigorous and informed, shaped by the city as few other minds are in the rest of Africa'. Working across a range of genres, he indulges in casual highbrow references, while, to quote again from Nkosi's obituary, 'fus[ing] into the English language the township idiom and re-juvenat[ing] tired words with an extreme imagery deriving from a life of danger and violence' (Nkosi 1972: viii). This 'rejuvenated' English is exemplified in the photo-story, 'Baby Come Duze' (1955), which featured pictures by Gopal S. Naransamy, and in which Themba presents 'the new lingo in the townships, bright as the bright-boys, made of Afrikaans, Zulu, Sotho, English and Brand-New Words' (Themba 2001 [1955]: 109).

Themba's association with *Drum* began after he won its first short story competition with 'Mob Passion' (1953) – a tragedy in the style of *Romeo and Juliet* in which a tryst on a train is brought to an abrupt halt by the violent schisms he saw apartheid producing through its ethic divide-and-rule policies. When presented with his prize by Mr Drum (Henry Nxumalo), Themba apparently said of his practice: 'I ... walk up and down the streets for hours, forming stories in the back of my mind. Then when I come to write them down, they are in one piece ready to be written' (qtd. Gray 2006: ix). This compositional *flâneurie* that stages 'the two-way encounter between mind and city' (Sheringham 1996: 111) was made possible by Themba's beloved Sophiatown, which remains an alluring mythos of black urbanity;[18] it was, declares Rob Nixon (1994: 12), 'more than just a place. It came to name an era and a departed style of life'.

Exempted from the 1923 Native Urban Areas Act restricting black freehold tenure, Sophiatown entered the 'fabulous decade' as one of the few areas in which Africans retained property rights in the city, along with Alexandra. Although it was in actuality largely inhabited by tenants, the promise of permanency was a significant part of its appeal, as was its proximity to the city centre and its porosity. These all distinguished Sophiatown from the compounds, and the townships modelled upon them, which imposed restrictive and alienating structures on black urban life. Anthony Sampson (2005 [1956]: 196), who served as the first editor of *Drum*, observed of Sophiatown that, 'alone of the African townships, it was part of Johannesburg ... There was no fence around Sophiatown ... and no policemen to examine permits at the gate'. In his 'Requiem for Sophiatown' (1959), written after the 'government had razed [it] to the ground, rebuilt it ... and resettled it with whites' (Themba 1972a: 6), Themba retrospectively locates its 'magic' in its way of being 'different and itself':

> You have the right to listen to the latest jazz records at Ah Sing's over the road. You can walk a coloured girl of an evening down to the Odin Cinema and no questions asked. You can try out Rhugubar's curry with your bare fingers without embarrassment. All this with no sense of heresy. Indeed, I've shown quite a few white people 'the little Paris of the Transvaal'.
>
> (Themba 1972 [1959]: 107)

Sophiatown's cosmopolitan culture was for Themba, as for many others, embodied in the jazz singer Dolly Rathebe, the 'spangled, glitter-spattered star' (Themba 1985 [1957]: 188) of the film *Jim Comes to Jo'burg*.[19] In his five-part profile, 'The Life and Love of Dolly Rathebe' (1957), Themba recalls also her career as *Drum* pin-up, including the sensational photoshoot by Jürgen Schadenberg in which she posed in a makeshift bikini contrived out of headscarves and handkerchiefs on a Johannesburg mine dump. The visual pun surfaces the hidden, underground labour that produced the conditions for a white leisure culture which came to centre upon annual pilgrimages to the seaside.[20] These images that *Drum* circulated through 'the little Paris of the Transvaal' anticipate also the slogan of the 1968 demonstrations in Paris: 'the beach beneath the street' (see Wark 2011). Indeed, whether on foot or by pen, Themba's movements through Sophiatown exemplify *avant la lettre* the associated Situationist practice of '*dérive*', or 'drifting', as a way of inhabiting the city while subverting its authoritarian structures and sidestepping the claims that capitalism has staked on it. Much of Rathebe's allure is in turn related to her refusal of the productive and oppressive roles assigned to black women by white capital and the apartheid state: 'from the beginning she was different from the domestic-servant, factory-working type of girl', Themba (1985 [1957]: 181) gushes: 'She saw herself as an artist and she just wouldn't go to work. Not for a white man, that is'.

Drum also regularly featured urban gangsters (or *'tsotsis'*) who styled themselves on American *film noir* and who became the ambiguous heroes of a culture responding to the criminalisation of black urbanity: increasing state regulation through the 1950s saw hundreds of thousands imprisoned each year; to be black in the city meant '[l]iving precariously' and enjoying at best a 'half-legal life' (Themba 1972 [1961]: 111, 109). *Drum* took up this predicament in various ways. Nxumalo's exposé of gaol conditions in 'Mr Drum Goes to Prison' (1954) was enabled by it: all he need do to be detained was to walk down the street without his pass.[21] In a prior account, 'Birth of a Tsotsi' (1951), Nxumalo had argued that apartheid policing produces rather than restrains criminality. While this early piece still holds the gangster at a distance, subsequent representations by him and other *Drum* writers are more equivocal or even approving. For all the predations they visit on black communities, *tsotsis* are admired for showing up the immorality of the apartheid legal order and for beating racial capitalism at its own game.[22] A number of stories in the magazine – such Bloke Modisane's 'The Dignity of Begging' (1951) and Maimane's hard-boiled series 'Crime for Sale' (1953) – also feature trickster characters who appropriate the tools of surveillance or play on the codes of the city in order to accumulate capital illicitly in ironic mimicry and inversion of an exclusionary and extractive state.[23] Modisane (1986 [1963]: 137–138) later remarked that his 'heroes were social maladjusts in a society where heroism is measured by acts of defiance against law and order'.

If the outlaw is a privileged figure of this 'fugitive' imagination, the shebeen (or illegal drinking-house) is its *locus classicus*. In autobiography and fiction, the shebeen is presented as a portal to urbanity: Abrahams's Leah in *Mine Boy* welcomes Xuma into her drinking-house where she teaches him city-ways and from which she supports an extended urban 'family' of affiliates; and, in his autobiography, *Blame Me on History*, Modisane (1986 [1963]: 35) records how his mother paid for his education by brewing beer. For Nkosi (2016 [1965]: 27) the shebeen is nothing less than 'the focal point of city life'; Themba and Nat Nakasa celebrate Sophiatown's famous drinking-holes over a number of reports and reflections; and, Motsisi tenders 'shebeen anecdotes' in his *Drum* column 'On the Beat' (1958–1959).

The shebeen and its avatars emerge in this literature as a counter-public sphere in which cityness is entered and claimed; it is the agora of characters who have been excluded from what Jürgen Habermas designates as the 'liberal public sphere' of 'rational-critical debate' (Habermas 1989), and black writers return to it at various points in the unfolding story of the South

African city. As Alex la Guma (1967 [1962]: 13) observes in a novella set in District Six (Cape Town's version of Sophiatown), when a character escapes into a drinking-hole after a humiliating encounter with a white policeman: '[t]he pub, like pubs all over the world, was a place for debate and discussion ... It was a forum, a parliament, a fountain of wisdom and a cesspool of nonsense'.

In the 'age of wisdom ... [and] foolishness', Sophiatown was memorialised by its writers almost as if it were a shebeen writ large – or 'the stuff that dreams are made of' (Themba 1959 [1972]: 104). But the claim to the city that it bespoke slipped away as the 'season of hope' was overcome by 'the winter of despair', and Themba's 'crepuscular' moment shades into night (Themba 1972a: 5). As the decade wore on, segregationist legislation strangled the vibrant urbanity that he had celebrated: the Group Areas Act of 1950 that formally instituted urban apartheid would go on to effect one of the largest forced removals of modern history;[24] the duplicitously named Natives (Abolition of Passes and Coordination of Documents) Act of 1952 replaced the old passbooks with even more odious reference books, which were now also imposed on women;[25] and, the Native Resettlement Act of 1954 cleared the way for the removal of the cosmopolitan communities of Sophiatown, Newclare and Martindale (the 'Western Areas'). By the end of the decade, the homeland system instrumental to the state's policy of 'separate development' had been introduced, stripping black South Africans of their nationality altogether. On 21 March 1960, an anti-pass protest in the Witwatersrand township of Sharpeville, led by Robert Sobukwe of the recently formed Pan Africanist Congress, ended in a massacre when police opened fire, killing 69 unarmed protestors (three more died in a related protest at Langa in Cape Town). Needless to say, *Drum*'s coverage of the massacre was sombre; the 'insouciant attitude' (Themba 1985 [1961]: 115) that its writers had cultivated during the preceding years vanished from the literary landscape for decades to come.

Notes

1 Nuttall and Mbembe notably characterise Johannesburg as 'the elusive metropolis' (2015).

2 The retrospective account of the diggings in Daphne Rooke's novel *Diamond Jo* (1965) provides insight into how the development of the town of Kimberley provides a prototype for extractive colonial capital and its labour policies, including restrictions on movement and the instantiation of the labour compound. Flouting the representational orthodoxy of the contemporary popular mining novel that celebrates 'individual effort and enterprise' (Hofmeyr 1978: 11), Rooke holds the mining magnet up for scrutiny, showing his rise to riches to be based on lies and betrayal.

3 See, inter alia, Ross's *Concise History of South Africa* (2008: 70–71) and Beavon's geohistory in *Johannesburg: The Making and Shaping of the City* (2004: 285–300); the account presented in this section leans heavily on these studies.

4 The literature discussed in this section focuses on migrants from within the borders of South Africa and Lesotho, but Hugh Masekela's jazz classic, '*Stimela* (The Coal Train)' (1974) follows the 'choo-choo train' that delivered those who laboured 'deep, deep, deep down in the belly of the earth' as it winds across 'all the hinterland of Southern and Central Africa'.

5 Blackburn travelled to South Africa in 1892, and published exposés of the 'blackbirding' labour contracting system and the illicit liquor trade on the Rand (Gray 1991: x).

6 Plaatje's *Mhudi* was completed earlier, in approximately 1917, but was only published in 1930 (also by Lovedale Press; the presses' editorial interference has been documented by Couzens and Gray, who published an edition based on the archived manuscript in the Heinemann African Writers Series in 1978, reissued by Penguin in 2005).

7 For discussion of the satirical column that RRR Dhlomo penned in *The Bantu World* newspaper between 1933 and 1943, and which joins *Leaven* and Abrahams's *Mine Boy* in offering 'a more complex and ambiguous reading of the city-countryside dynamic' through an emphasis on 'urban survival and agency in a place that has become home', see Sandwith (2018: 19), who shows that urbanisation was represented in more tonally variant ways than admitted by many studies of the 'Jim comes to Joburg' theme.

8 Recorded by HJ van Zyl in 1941; this translation is from *Voices from Within: Black Poetry from South Africa* (Chapman and Dangor ed. 1982).

9 On the taxes introduced under colonial rule to push independent pastoralists into the cash economy, thus driving them to supply labour to the mines or face imprisonment, see Ndlovu (2017).

10 As Gunner (2008) finds in a study of post-apartheid *isicathamiya* performance, 'the genre … enables its users and their audiences to see both their own city and the cities of the world as inter-connected'.

11 For Maxeke's own analysis of the circumstances of African women in the colonial city, see her essay 'Social Conditions Among Bantu Women and Girls' (1930), introduced by Ntongela Masilela in the collection *Women Writing Africa: The Southern Region* (2003) (ed. Daymond et al.), 195–200.

12 Cover blurb on the Heinemann African Writers series edition published in 1963.

13 Mamdani (1996: 7) argues that British colonial rule in Africa introduced a bifurcation between city and countryside, and citizen and subject, that was deepened by the apartheid state, which instituted 'the forced removal of those marked unproductive so they may be pushed out of white areas back into native homelands and … the forced straddling of those deemed productive between workplace and homeland through an ongoing cycle of annual migrations'.

14 Nixon (1994: 261, n.78) refers to an interview in which 'Nkosi suggests that young male African viewers [of the film adaptation of *Cry, the Beloved Country*] identified with John Kumalo, the priest's activist, irremediably urban brother, despite Paton's negative portrayal of him'. See also Nkosi's commentary in 'The Fabulous Decade', which concludes: 'I suppose, in a sense, the war between us [the urbanites associated with *Drum* magazine] and Stephen Kumalo was … a war between two generations – the older generation, which looked forward to

fruitful changes under the Smuts government, and the young who saw themselves beginning their adult life under a more brutal apartheid regime' (Nkosi 2016 [1965]: 20).

15 See the selection from *Drum* in Chapman (ed.) (2001 [1989]). Themba's writing has also been anthologised in *The Will to Die* (ed. Stuart and Holland 1972), *The World of Can Themba* (ed. Patel, 1985) and *Requiem for Sophiatown* (ed. Gray 2006); I quote from the first two anthologies and have dated them with reference to Gray's 'Notes on Sources' in the latter.

16 See Driver (1996) for commentary on how this promotion of consumer culture was organised around – and sought to produce – the patriarchal nuclear family.

17 Established under the Bantu Authorities Act of 1951, the Bantustans consolidated the native reserves that functioned as labour reservoirs and dumping grounds to which surplus peoples – women, children, the old and the unproductive – were consigned. A continuation of colonial practices of land appropriation, mineral extraction and labour exploitation, they were also part of the apartheid state's more ambitious plan of social engineering and, ultimately, to strip black South Africans of citizenship altogether.

18 On post-apartheid returns to Sophiatown and the *Drum* decade, see Samuelson (2008, 2014b).

19 Themba's profile of Rathebe notably does not include her reference to the rural 'kraal' in his version of 'Jo'burg City Blues' (also called 'Golden City Blues'): 'Jo'burg City, the Golden City; What did I come here for?; Oh, Jo'burg City, the Golden City; I'm far away from my home' (in Themba 1985 [1953]: 187).

20 *Drum* otherwise shied clear of critiquing the mines; its proprietor, Jim Bailey, was the son of gold magnate Abe Bailey.

21 'Mr Drum Goes to Jail' ends with a set of recommendations prefaced by the observation that '*this account … describes nothing extraordinary. Most Africans living in town can expect to be sent to jail sometime during their lives*' (Nxumalo 2001 [1954]: 46; original emphasis).

22 See Fenwick (1996: 632): 'In the face of a white state that declared black urban living to be illegitimate, *Drum* turned to figures with which they could simultaneously demonstrate the true illegality that was the result of segregation, and the vibrancy, power and legitimacy of the black urban culture that housed them'.

23 In its initial form, published at the dawn of the 'fabulous decade', 'The Dignity of Begging' concludes with the narrator returning to the countryside (albeit with his Sophiatown piano); on republication in 1958, the ending was altered to admit the hold that the city continues to exert on him: 'Deep down I know that I will want it [the room in Sophiatown] again … I have to come back. I owe it to the profession' (qtd. Chapman 2001 [1989]: 201).

24 Researchers in the Surplus Peoples Project estimated that 3.5 million had suffered forced removal by 1982.

25 See 'Mothers of the Revolution' in Chapter 4 for discussion of women's resistance against pass laws, including the Women's March of 1956.

3

LIGHT CITY, DARK CITY

Electric lights! How beautiful they look from a distance ...
Standing here in a dark little world, viewing them from afar,
miles away, you know they are beyond your reach ... Here, a
dark township, Orlando; ... then far away, clusters and clusters of [light.]
      – Es'kia Mphahlele, *Down Second Avenue* (1959)

As segregation was increasingly entrenched, South African cities took a concentric shape: the central business district and its surrounding white suburbs were ringed by townships that reprised the mine compound function. Constructed as dormitory towns to house a population who were admitted to the city only in service, these 'locations', as they were also called, suffered constant state surveillance and were scoured by levels of deprivation deemed suitable for those declared to be mere 'sojourners' in urban space. The result was a hyperbolic instantiation of the colonial city as described by Frantz Fanon (1963 [1961]: 29): '[t]he settler's town is a well-fed town ... The native town is a hungry town, starved of bread, of meat, of shoes, of coal, of light'; 'divided into compartments' or 'cut in two', such cities manifest a 'Manichean' structure. Viewed from the darkened outskirts of the colonial-apartheid city, the electric lights that appear in a series of autobiographies and novels as synecdoche for 'the glamour of urban life' are increasingly received as symbolic of an 'indifferent, impersonal, hard and cold' state (Mphahlele 1959: 22, 205) – a state that sought to evict black South Africans from both cityness and citizenship.

Segregating cities and the 'tyranny of place'

A setting that generates so much pain as South Africa does
claims all our physical and emotional responses. You hold
on to it, document it, even though, or because it riles you

DOI: 10.4324/9781003174189-3

up ... And always you feel it absolutely necessary to give
an account of yourself, of how you grow up in such a setting ... From this you evolve an aesthetic.

    – Es'kia Mphahlele, *Down Second Avenue* (1959)

Autobiography, social realism and naturalism are the dominant genres of
a literature that sought to give an account of the claim that South Africa's
urban settings made on their authors during the early years of apartheid.
Reviewing its colonial genealogy from the vantage point of this period,
Abrahams's autobiographical *Tell Freedom* (1954) foregrounds the startling
disparities of the segregated city as his narrator traverses its partitions during the 1930s: 'the contrast was so great, I might as well have stepped into
another world, on another planet' (Abrahams 1954: 103). Feeling hemmed
in by the slum, he starts taking 'long lonely walks into the white areas of
Johannesburg', until he realises that 'these streets and trees, almost, the
clean air I breathed here, were: RESERVED FOR EUROPEANS ONLY'
(Abrahams 1954: 163–164). The act of 'walking in the city' is given a pecu-
liarly South African inflection: his movements curtailed, Abraham's narrator is unable to engage in the dialogue with its streets that 'the little Paris
of the Transvaal' briefly affords Themba; instead, he finds himself at the
receiving end of an injunctive monologue as signage shouts at him from
every corner. This is not a city that permits idle strolling or 'drifting' by
its black inhabitants; movements are instead required to be purposeful and
legitimated by the 'pieces of paper' that control 'a man's life' (Abrahams
1956: 180), foremost of which is the passbook or '*dompas*' (lit. dumb pass;
contraction of 'domestic passport') that restricts black claims on the city.

    Set two decades later, Gordimer's novel *A World of Strangers* (1958) is
plotted across the divisions of the early apartheid city. Whites are shown
'sated with comforts' while Africans suffer material deprivation, though
Gordimer (1962 [1958]: 77, 80) also presents the former as having superficial lives and being too afraid to walk the streets at night. The protagonist,
the Englishman Toby, befriends two Sophiatown denizens, Steven and Sam,
who are based on the *Drum* writers Themba and Todd Matshikiza; he is
partly modelled on the editor Anthony Sampson. Toby shuttles between the
'unreality' of the wealthy suburbs and the satisfying social contact offered
by the slums, but his friendship with the black men is ultimately thwarted
by 'the awful triumphant separateness of the place' (Gordimer 1962 [1958]:
110, 203). The metaphor that the novel reaches for is apposite: like train-
tracks, the lives of black and white are said to 'run parallel', the machinery
of apartheid being marshalled to 'preventing a crossing' (Gordimer 1962
[1958]: 115). When Steven is killed in a car crash while fleeing a police raid

28

on an Indian club, the deathly character of segregation becomes apparent. The narrative concludes indecisively on a railway platform: Sam bids Toby farewell, convinced the Englishman will not come back to Johannesburg, though he vows to return; friendship across the lines of the segregating city is thus proposed in only the most provisional manner.

Dedicated to the son of its protagonist, who would – at the time of its composition – suffer endorsement out of the city, Modikwe Dikobe's *The Marabi Dance* (1973),[1] like Abraham's *Tell Freedom*, recreates the slum-yards of inner-city Johannesburg in the 1930s from the vantage point of an increasingly repressive state. The demand to produce passes grows volu-minously across the narrative, underscoring the growing precarity of black urban life. Concerned with the vulnerability of unorganised labour, the novel culminates in a call to unionise. But, unlike in *Mine Boy*, labour solidarity is no longer sufficient to cut across what is by now an entrenched racial divide, while the kind of liberalism espoused in *Cry, the Beloved Country* is seen as a ruse to extract ever more from Africans before expelling them from urban life. The state directs the action of the closing chapters in which Martha, the protagonist, is removed from another inner-city area of Johannesburg to Orlando in the recently established South Western Townships (contracted into 'Soweto') – the township from which Mphahlele will later view the distant lights of the city proper. The train now becomes a dominant figure in the narrative as relocated subjects are consigned to a life of commuting that they can ill afford (a complaint asserted also in the bus boycotts in which the author was involved).[2] On one such journey, Martha passes a platform on which a group of migrants is assembled to return to the reserves, and wonders whether they are going back to die, as many indeed did – and still do – after contracting silicosis on the mines.

If the train conveys the meaning of the novel's bleak conclusion, the motorcar anticipates it early in the narrative. As occurs also in *Mine Boy* as part of its critique of segregated streets, a minor character is knocked over by a car in a scene catalysing the subsequent events of *The Marabi Dance*; in *A World of Strangers*, as we have seen, the urbane character Sam is killed in a crash that signifies the ruination of associational city life. Symbolically, then, these novels encode car and train as metonyms of the 'Manichean' city and its duplicitous promise of modernity – and invest both with appre-hensions of death.

In *Down Second Avenue* (1959), Mphahlele charts the growing factures across the city while weaving the story of self into a biography of Marabastad (located near the centre of Pretoria, Marabastad like Sophiatown and District Six, housed a diverse population before its inhabitants were relo-cated to racially exclusive townships). Concerned with affirming humanity and bearing witness to the 'drama of survival', Mphahlele emphasises the ways in which a sense of 'community' once nurtured '[a]round the communal fire' has been transported into this strange new world of '[a]venues and streets' (Mphahlele 1959: 34; see Gaylard 2004: 274). Though they are the deprived dark face of the 'city of light' (Mandela 1994a: 51), the slums are shown to be animated by what a theorist of the African city, AbdouMaliq Simone (2008), has called 'people as infrastructure' – an enabling assemblage that is intimated by a suggestive image in the story 'Lesane' when gossip is said to have 'shot up and down Nadia Street like electric current' (Mphahlele 2001 [1956b]: 133). The human 'conjunctions' (Simone 2008) cherished in Mphahlele's writing stand in contrast to the detachment or 'indifference' that Simmel (2004 [1903]: 15) locates in metropolitan modernity, and which Mphahlele identifies with the 'hard and cold' white city. They come to support instead the emergence of what Mbembe and Nuttall (2008: 9) have described as the 'Afropolis': the city as the locale of the 'African modern'.

This is, however, not to say that the urban landscape which Mphahlele paints is idealised. That these are stunting and dehumanising settings is everywhere emphasised. In so doing, *Down Second Avenue* begins to elaborate an idea that Mphahlele defines as 'the tyranny of place' and through which he reflects on what he perceives as black South African writers' attachment to the location of their dispossession. This idea is expressed formally as much as stated in the autobiography: the interludes that interrupt the chronological narrative, breaking often into the present tense, convey the immediacy and inescapability of the pain generated by the setting that he recreated in retrospect from exile. 'I have been moving up and down Second Avenue since I was born' (Mphahlele 1959: 159) is the lament uttered in one of these interludes.

Mphahlele (2002 [1973]) comments further in his critical writing on the aesthetic that has evolved from 'the tyranny of place'. Among his examples is La Guma's novella, *A Walk in the Night* (1962), which, as he notes elsewhere, 'documents the setting in all its sordid and oppressive detail to show how human character can be held hostage, ravaged, or even exiled, by the political and economic structures determined by a ruling class' (Mphahlele 1983: 15). J.M. Coetzee (1992 [1974]: 352) observes similarly of La Guma's novella that '[p]aragraphs are given over to fascinated catalogues of "ordinary life"' whose 'repetitiveness' testifies to the author's 'horror of a degraded world'. The neighbourhood itemised in these inventories is Cape Town's District Six, which, like Sophiatown, became symbolic of a heterodox cosmopolitanism nestled within the colonial-apartheid city. Yet, in contrast to many portrayals of Sophiatown and the District, *A Walk in the Night* is purposefully unromanticised, indicting the sordid circumstances in which black South Africans were forced to live under apartheid. To this end, Coetzee (1992 [1974]: 345) finds that it employs a 'naturalistic-deterministic' mode, 'its large cast of negligible characters driven to various fates by social forces beyond their understanding'. It does, however, shift from disgusted documentation to anticipatory symbolism in a conclusion in which 'creaming waves' pound relentlessly 'against the granite citadels of rock' (La Guma 1967 [1962]: 96) as if to portend that natural forces – or the transoceanic traffic they convey – will inevitably erode the walls encasing the enclaved cities through which the regime pursued its vision of 'separate development' (see Samuelson 2016a: 529–530).

The 'tyranny of place' asserts itself again in La Guma's subsequent novel, *And a Threefold Cord* (1964), which is set in the desolate townships that were being established on the far outskirts of Cape Town as the city proper was claimed for 'whites only'. The enforced alienation of those dispatched to this wasteland is demonstrated in a demeaning night raid for passbooks. Social realism cuts close to the absurd when a man, stepping into his yard in his pyjamas, is detained even as he protests that his pass is in the room a few feet behind him. All the while, the rain beats down incessantly, reminding that those who have been denied the right to inhabit the centre have been exiled onto a floodplain.

Writing in the ruins

Ons Pola Hier
– Graffiti, *Sophiatown* (1956)

You are now in fairyland
– Graffiti, *District Six* (1970)

When Sophiatown was designated for 'whites only' under the Group Areas Act, and its African residents were removed to Meadowlands in Soweto, a phrase in the inner-city polyglot was scrawled on one of its condemned walls: '*Ons pola hier*' ('We're staying here'). Although ultimately unsuccessful, it lay claim to what Lefebvre identifies as the right to reimagine the city as both domicile and creative work produced collectively by and for its inhabitants. After the destruction of Sophiatown, the phrase lived on in the chorus to the popular jazz song 'Meadowlands' that was composed by Strike Vilakazi during the removals of 1956: '*Ons daak nie, ons pola hier ... We're not moving, we're staying here*'. Similarly with the words written across the entrance to Cape Town's District Six – another area that was ostensibly subject to slum clearance but which was understood to have been condemned due to the challenge that its cosmopolitan composition posed to the apartheid ideal of 'separate development': the graffiti 'You are now in fairyland' was used as an epigraph in Rive's novel *'Buckingham Palace', District Six* (1986), and provides also the title of one of Dawid Kramer and Talip Petersen's musicals, *Fairyland* (1989).

Razed along with the structures accommodating black urban life, and displaying these claims on the city, were places steeped in personal and collective memory. This, along with the flight of writers into exile, accounts for the rise of autobiography, which by the 1960s had bypassed the short story and journalism as the privileged genre of black writing. Todd Matshikiza in *Chocolates for My Wife* (1961), Modisane in *Blame Me on History* (1963) and, later, Don Mattera in *Memory Is the Weapon* (1987),[3] for instance, take up memoir to reconstruct dismantled dwellings and recollect dispersed communities. The tone is often elegiac and infused with melancholy. Modisane's autobiography opens: 'Something in me died, a piece of me died, with the dying of Sophiatown' (Modisane 1986 [1963]: 5).

Many other inner-city 'black spots' were declared 'white' during this period, such as Fordsburg in Johannesburg from which the writer Ahmed Essop was removed in 1963. In *The Hajji & Other Stories* (1967), he uses the form of the short story cycle to express the tension between the 'centripetal' force of community, on the one hand, and the 'centrifugal' force of the dissembling state, on the other hand (Marais 1995: 29).[4] Though apparently an Indian enclave, Essop's Fordsburg is shown to be in constant dialogue with the surrounding city: its residents move in and out of the familiar quarter and members of other groups enter and engage with its inhabitants. Yet, while Fordsburg's conviviality is rendered elegiacally, the collection also offers satirical self-critique of a community that Essop shows to be sometimes complicit in apartheid's hierarchies. An example of this can be found in the titular story: after being assaulted by white youth for failing to take the separate lift designated for 'non-whites' when visiting his pass-for-white brother in Hillbrow, the eponymous hero regains his 'self-possession' in the 'non-white' train compartment where he finds himself 'among people who respected him' (Essop 1986 [1967]: 6).

The last two stories in *The Hajji* are set after the forced removals. The locale changes abruptly from Fordsburg to the newly constructed Lenasia township that was assigned to Johannesburg's Indian population, and which lies some 35km from the city centre. Gone are the characters that readers have come to know; gone too is the atmosphere with which they have grown familiar: it is as if the collection itself imparts the dislocation wrought by the mandatory move along with the barrenness of the new habitation. The train too has changed tracks as the now-lengthy commutes to the city are loaded with oppressive signs of militarism and homogeneity.

In Gordimer's *A World of Strangers*, tentative hope and anticipated disappointment met on the railway platform. But such undecided conclusions seem no longer available to writers after the destruction of Sophiatown and the Sharpeville Massacre. Trains now become unequivocally dystopian. The change can be charted across Themba's writing: in 'Mob Passion' (1953), the train carries a claim to modernity by providing a haven for romantic encounters that elicit an individualised rather than communal subject;[5] in the later nonfictional 'Dube Train' (1964), the 'congested' carriage that is now 'filled with sour-smelling humanity' (Themba 1964 [1972]: 57) conveys instead the defeat and degradation of the 'city of dreams'.[6]

Bulldozers also begin to enter the literary scene as vehicles of a scarred and haunted cityscape. In Sipho Sepamla's poem 'The Start of a Removal' (1975), for instance, their 'drone' (Sepamla 1975: 40) provides the soundtrack to the destruction of urban conviviality, replacing the orchestral 'throbbing from the bowels of the earth, from the mouths and hearts of men, from the machines' that Abraham's Xuma had found in the golden city. Writing from Cape Town, James Matthews protests against the '[m]echanical monsters' that 'ravished' the 'beauty of district six', while the 'melancholy mew' of a 'solitary seagull' recalls the now 'effaced' expansiveness that the prospect over the port had offered its residents.[7] In the collection *Bulldozer* (1983), Achmat Dangor presents a sequence in Kaaps, the creolised dialect of the Cape underclass, that mocks the regulation of inner-city residents into the 'straight paths and wide lanes of propriety' of the grid-patterned townships constructed on the urban periphery (Dangor 1983: 63; my translation). In *Waiting for Leila* (published as a short story in 1980 and as a novella in the subsequent year), he conjures 'ineradicable' (Dangor 1981) ghosts among the ruins of the District. Here, spectrality becomes a mode of repossessing urban space.

The most famous chronicle of District Six, and of its destruction, is Rive's *'Buckingham Palace', District Six*. Almost a fictionalised biography of the tenement flats in which Rive was raised, its refrain is: '*We must never forget ...*' The three sections of the novel are prefaced by a frame narrator who summons up razed structures and repopulates them, animating abandoned buildings with the sounds, smells and stories of their expelled residents. Written after the demolitions, which had started in 1966 and were concluded by the mid-1970s, *'Buckingham Palace'* is certainly nostalgic, but it is self-consciously so. Its retrospective gaze lingers appreciatively over a cosmopolitanism that it holds in counterpoint to the segregated city in order to claim the District as 'an island in a sea of apartheid' (Rive 1986: 96). While Rive elsewhere acknowledges that it was 'a ripe, raw and rotten slum', he nonetheless treasures it for being 'both urban and urbane' (Rive 1990: 112). As his character, Zoot, puts it: '[w]e knew that District Six was dirty and rotten. Their newspapers told us that often enough. But they didn't say that it was also warm and friendly. That it contained humans. That it was never a place – that it was a people' (Rive 1986: 198). The novel *'Buckingham Palace'* compiles an alternative archive to that of the white-owned media, one that is based on the memories of the District's displaced residents and which appreciates the human 'infrastructure' that – as Simone (2008) finds in his studies of African cities – enables many apparently dysfunctional urban spaces to work.

Refuse, recycling and refusal

> We're whiteman's rubbish. That's why he's so *beneukt* with us. He can't get rid of his rubbish. He throws it away, we pick it up. Wear it. Sleep in it. Eat it. We're made of it now. His rubbish is people.
>
> – Athol Fugard, *Boesman & Lena* (1969/1978)

Cities are often conceived as theatres of consumption. So too in South Africa; but in the apartheid city, the thematic of waste and disposability, and of recycling and repossession, comes strongly to the fore. It is pronounced in Athol Fugard's existential drama *Boesman & Lena* (1969/1978),[8] which plays out on the wastelands surrounding the provincial city of Port Elizabeth. As Fugard (1978: vii, viii) notes, it was informed by the urban setting (with its 'social strata' ranging 'from total affluence on the white side to the extremest poverty on the non-white') as well as by a period he spent working as a clerk in a Native Commissioner's Court that heard pass-law offenses; here he 'saw more suffering than [he] could cope with' and 'began to understand how [his] country functioned'. *Boesman & Lena* bears bitter testimony to both. The eponymous characters walk onto the empty stage loaded with detritus, and the action revolves around their futile efforts to locate themselves in a world that has jettisoned them. Recycling becomes the leitmotif: repeatedly circling a city that has thrown them away as if they themselves were refuse, the characters recommission its trash. Lena tries to give order to the sequence of their movements in an effort to orient herself, but her appeal to Boesman is met with the brusque response: 'What? Find yourself?' (Fugard 1978 [1969/1973]: 252). The play asks the same question: how, indeed, can Lena locate herself in a place of prescribed dislocation and in which she herself has been disposed of? The commodities in which she and Boesman deal on the margins of the city are symbolic of their predicament: the 'empties' they collect to exchange for cash (and more drink) signify their own discarded status.

In *Sizwe Bansi Is Dead* (1972), which Fugard produced collaboratively with John Kani and Winston Ntshona, the act of recycling turns refuse more emphatically into refusal, and the arresting pass office that informed the genesis of Fugard's playwrighting is replaced by the more ambivalent setting of the photographic studio.[9] While helping to ensnare black subjects in the bureaucracy of influx control regulations (the imposed reference books included an ID photo), it also offers a space in which they lay their own claim on the city. When a new client, Robert Zwelinzima, arrives in his studio, the proprietor Styles composes him against a backdrop depicting the 'City of the Future' that is painted on the verso of a world atlas. Zwelinzima has, however, been endorsed out of the city and seemingly out of a viable future: he has effectively been condemned to starvation in the homeland to which he has been assigned. But when he and Styles stumble upon a pass-bearing corpse in the street, Robert Zwelinzima is able to insert his photograph into this 'Book of Life', thus assuming the identity of the dead man, Sizwe Bansi (Fugard, Kani & Ntshona 1972: 181). Urban life under apartheid, suggests the play, demands an erasure of identity and the performance of predetermined parts. Such roles are, however, susceptible to subversion in their iterative performance (another mode of recycling), as evidenced in a *mise-en-abyme* of play-acting that erupts spontaneously on the shopfloor of a car-tyre manufacturer; they can also be 'styled' into a claim on the city in the momentary pause before the camera shutter closes.

Equally concerned with the performance of urban subjectivity in scenes of constraint and disposal is Miriam Tlali's novel *Muriel at Metropolitan* (1979). Completed in the late 1960s and issued in different editions in 1975 and 1979,[10] *Muriel* is the first novel in English by a black South African woman to be published in the country. The setting is a hire-purchase retail store through which Tlali simultaneously denounces white capitalism and admits black urban aspirations: the shop exploits black city-dwellers while stocking the accessories with which they hold at bay the dehumanising effects of apartheid. Demonstrating how the apartheid city exploits Africans as consumers, and not only as labour, Tlali exposes an industry that entices customers into purchases they cannot afford: a key function of Metropolitan Radios is the repossession of partly paid-off appliances and furnishings when their owners default on the terms of purchase. The novel does not, however, present black consumers simply as duped naïfs; they are instead shown to be asserting their own claims on the city and refusing their assigned place as 'temporary sojourners'.

One customer bemoans: 'Living in the townships is like living on shifting sands. Every Parliamentary session brings in fresh, more oppressive laws ... Sometimes I wonder why we bother to buy furniture at all' (Tlali 1979: 169). Observes Muriel: 'I suppose like people the world over, we want to feel that we possess something. We need something firm to hold onto' (Tlali 1979: 169). Apartheid exacerbates the modern predicament in which, to quote Marshall Berman's (1988) redirection of Karl Marx's memorable phrase, 'all that is solid melts into air'. The insecurity of black urban tenure that is imposed by this oppressive state stokes the desire for something secure with which to anchor subjectivity, but the irony is that the apparently solid things procured to this end literarily melt into air when they are repossessed. In the face of the vanishing dream of black urban modernity, the destruction of Sophiatown – 'our Sophiatown' (Tlali 1979: 123) – is recalled by the novel as emblematic.

The primary commodity sold in Metropolitan Radios is significant. Broadcasting in nine different languages, the Radio Bantu service of the South African Broadcasting Corporation (SABC) aimed 'to bolster the apartheid regime's vision of ethnically authentic and separate cultural identity' (Barnard 2007: 133). In Tlali's novel, however, SABC listeners switch back and forth between channels in subversive auditory receptions of this state apparatus. Intended to maintain rural allegiances during what the ruling regime sought to limit to mere sojourns in the city, radio instead comes to function as a connective and mobilising technology that produces imaginative interactions between the city and countryside (Coplan 1985: 161).[11] This quotidian refusal of grand apartheid's efforts to 'de-urbanise' and 're-tribalise' black South Africans is evident across the literature. In a retrospective account of his childhood in an apartheid township, Jacob Dlamini (2009: 31), for instance, recalls how, '[i]n a political time and space that was coded in racial terms, with severe limits imposed on black mobility, black people could move through radio in ways that the apartheid state could not curtail'.

While in *Muriel at Metropolitan* the hire-purchase store stages the scenario of a city 'divided into two worlds' (1979: 11),[12] in Yvonne Burgess's *A Life to Live* (1973) a second-hand clothing shop and a grand residence turned deteriorating boarding-house provide the setting from which impoverished whites lay their competing claim on the city during the Great Depression of the 1930s.[13] It is, oppressively, an exclusive claim. Framed by the degrading circumstances of their poverty, the occupants of the boarding-house find an outlet for their frustrations in enactments of racial power that range from the banal to the brutal. Reaching towards the National Party victory in the elections of 1948, the novel provides – from the perspective of the 1970s – an aetiology of apartheid as a response to what the 1932 Carnegie Commission report deemed to be the 'poor white problem' and which was seen to threaten white supremacy. (The report recommended segregation and white job reservation, which the apartheid state was later to offer through the railways, in the interests of 'uplifting' impoverished Afrikaners and thus avoiding 'miscegenation' and race 'embarrassment'.)[14] When the protagonist, Nel, returns to the countryside, worn out and discarded like the clothing that she has spent her life peddling in the second-hand store, she finds that her people have gentrified and see her as a shameful reminder of their prior poverty and of the blurred racial boundaries it had permitted. The novel, in turn, reviews the process of gentrification from the perspective of the segregated present in order to shame certain readers with a reminder of the practices of mutual assistance that enabled the poor – both black and white – to survive the depression.

In contrast to those elevated by the state, Africans 'returning' to the countryside during the 1970s – that is, during the period of the novel's production – find instead the depleted conditions from which the young Nel had fled some decades before. Apartheid ushered in a time of plenty for its white citizens, both rural and urban. Its black subjects, in contrast, were thrust into a seemingly interminable depression as they were 'endorsed out' of cities and forcibly removed to over-crowded and underdeveloped 'homelands'. These are the tribulations that concern *The Long Journey of Poppie Nongena* (1978/1980), which testifies to a woman's struggle to maintain herself and her family in the city rather than submit to such sentencing.[15]

Poppie Nongena is an ostensibly collaborative work: the named author, the Afrikaans novelist Elsa Joubert, entered into an agreement with her domestic worker (the real-life prototype of the fictive Poppie) to write her story and to share with her the royalties that would arise from its publication.[16] The employee's motive was apparently to earn enough money to buy her own house in the city. The realisation of this desire for a stable domestic matrix – for a home of one's own – may well have been Poppie's ultimate achievement, but it was most often only as domestic workers in white women's homes that black women were able to maintain a claim on the city. Rather than holding them apart, the segregated city thus binds women into intimate relations of dependency and exploitation. As Mphahlele's short story 'Mrs Plum' (2006 [1967]: 165) earlier observed: the so-called white suburbs with their ubiquitous domestic servants and gardeners were, in fact, 'full of blackness'.

Poppie's story underlines also the gendered nature of the state policies that sought to consign black South Africans to the rural reserves. Although she is 'townborn', her marriage to a migrant labourer from the Ciskei at a time when passbooks had been imposed on women as well as men means that she fails to qualify for residence in the Cape and is 'returned' to a 'homeland' that she has never seen before, while her country-born husband is permitted to remain in the city for as long as his labour is required.[17] Poppie's unwavering efforts to secure the right to live in Cape Town are described in laborious detail as the pass office moves to the forefront of her existence, becoming the organising centre of her story. Eventually, despite her persistence, she is sent 'back' to live with her husband's family, they themselves having already been evicted from their land and moved into a cramped state-controlled 'village'. 'I felt, really, I'm now quite thrown away' (Joubert 1980 [1978]: 200), she reflects.

When Poppie is finally able to return to the city, the townships are erupting with the 'revolt of the children' as the youth insurrection that ignited in Soweto on 16 June 1976 spreads to Cape Town. Initially, she is unsettled by the disruption of generational hierarchies that she had experienced as stable in the countryside, and she is further dismayed when 'city-borners' clash with a group variously called the 'homelanders', 'migrants' and the '*amagoduka*' ('the Xhosa name for the migrants that come to the cities for work and then return to the land') (Joubert 1980 [1978]: 324, 326). But she comes to appreciate that the children's militancy is their only possible response to the assault that is being directed at the 'people of the location' by the combined forces of the 'riot squad' and 'the migrants' (Joubert 1980: 332).[18] Ceding to 'the children's' authority, she (and perhaps also Joubert) understands that the younger generation is redefining the township as a site of struggle precisely by receiving it as yet another form of enclosure. This insight is expressed with piercing acuity in a declaration by one of 'the children' that she approvingly quotes, and which both echoes and also offers an advance on her earlier recognition that she has been 'thrown away': 'Let the roof of the gaol cover the whole of the location, let the whole of the location become a gaol, because, why, we are born to die' (Joubert 1980 [1978]: 353).

Notes

1 The narrative was completed a decade before, and edited by Lionel Abrahams and others before publication in 1973; it was released under a pseudonym, since its author – Marks Rammitloa – was banned for his trade union activities, following his involvement in the bus boycotts and squatter movements of the 1940s.

2 Kruger (2013: 68) describes his short story 'We Shall Walk' as a 'lightly fictionalized account' of the bus boycott that takes its name from the declamation: 'they want six-pence for bus fare and so the people walk'.

3 Published internationally as *Gone with the Twilight: A Story of Sophiatown* (1987).

4 'As a form positioned somewhere between the coherence of the novel proper and the disconnectedness of the "mere" collection of autonomous short stories, the short fiction cycle evinces a dualism which renders it particularly well suited to the representation of that tension between centripetal and centrifugal or entropic impulses which obtains in any society. It is a form especially apposite to the South Africa context, where the conflict between community, solidary and national unity, on the one hand, and dissociation, segregation and "apartheid", on the other, is notorious' (Marais 1995: 29).

5 For analysis of 'Mob Passion', see Samuelson (2008: 66–68).
6 Dube is part of South Western Townships in which residents of the Western Areas were resettled. As Gray notes (2006: xv), 'Dube Train' is a reworking of 'Terror in the Trains', which was published in *Drum* in 1957 after the forced removals from Sophiatown; the earlier version places emphasis on inter-ethnic violence, concluding: 'The situation has been aggravated … by the policy of ethnic grouping, which has led the more tribal among us to think of other tribes as 'foreigners', 'enemies'. We are not allowed to learn to live together in peace, say the train-using, bus-boarding philosophers to whom the Dube wave of terror has become a matter of life and death' (Themba 1957 [1972]: 70–71).
7 Published in the *Cape Times* (qtd. Hart 1990).
8 The play premiered in 1969 in Grahamstown with Fugard in the role of Boesman and Yvonne Bryceland playing Lena (and Glynn Day as Outa), and the play-script was copyrighted in 1973, when a film version directed by Ross Devenish and starring Fugard and Bryceland was also released.
9 First performed at The Space theatre in Cape Town in 1972, with Fugard as director, Kani playing Styles and Ntshona in the roles of Sizwe Bansi and Bantu, *Sizwe Bansi Is Dead* was televised for the BBC in 1974 (directed by John Davies) and for CBS in 1981 (directed by Merril Brockway).
10 Its delayed and double publication is related to perceived editorial controls over black writing and to black women's minority status under apartheid, which meant that Tlali could not enter into a publication contract; the version of the novel discussed here is that which Tlali declared to be 'the integral text' (see Samuelson 2012: 763).
11 See also the film *African Jim* in which Jim yearns nostalgically for his rural homestead after hearing traditional music on the airwaves, and yet translates this longing into a jazz performance that instead proclaims his presence in 'Joburg City'.
12 An alternative title for the novel was *Between Two Worlds*.
13 My thanks to Kelwyn Sole for drawing my attention to this novel.
14 *The Poor White Problem in South Africa: Report of the Carnegie Commission* (5 vols), authored by R.W. Wilcocks et al. (1932).
15 The book was first published in Afrikaans in 1978 and translated into English by Joubert and her husband as *The Long Journey of Poppie Nongena* in 1980 (the title of some later editions is simply 'Poppie' or 'Poppie Nongena').
16 See McClintock (1995: 299–300) for the terms of collaboration, including 'Poppie Nongena's' intention to purchase a house with the royalties that accrued to her, and Joubert (in Joubert and Meyer 2006) for the disclosure that 'Poppie Nongena' was actually a woman named Eunice Msutwana who was employed as her domestic worker.
17 The Ciskei was one of two 'states' designated for Xhosas under the Bantu Authorities Act of 1951 and which were named 'homelands' or 'Bantustans' under the Promotion of Bantu Self-Government Act of 1959 (there were altogether ten Bantustans designated to different ethnic groups). The Bantu Homelands Citizenship Act of 1970 completed the legislative process of stripping black South Africans of their citizenship and investing it instead in the puppet-governments of the homelands.
18 The distinguishing white armbands and headbands mark the 'migrants' as the state-sponsored vigilante group known as the '*witdoeke*' (lit. white cloths); see the discussion of J.M. Coetzee's *Age of Iron* in Chapter 4.

4

RESISTANT CITIES

Black man, you are on your own.
– Steve Bantu Biko, *I Write What I Like* (1978 [1969])

The most potent weapon in the hands of the oppressor is the
mind of the oppressed.
– Steve Bantu Biko, *I Write What I Like* (1978 [1971])

The Black Consciousness Movement exerted a profound politico-aesthetic
influence on literary claims on the city from the late 1960s onwards. Its
philosophy emphasised psychological liberation and self-reliance and,
although it was itself largely urban in membership and experience, it
encouraged the reclamation of African histories rooted in the countryside.
Writing under the nom-de-plume Frank Talk, its founder, Steve Bantu
Biko, published a series of articles that set the tone for black writing of the
period: defiantly forging its own standards and asserting its own purpose
(his collected writing was posthumously published under the bold title 'I
write what I like' after he was killed by police while in custody in 1977).
Igniting the militancy of 'the children' that *Poppie Nongena* records, the
Black Consciousness Movement also informed a literature of confrontation
and reprisal that was infused with a 'language of urgency' (Mtshali 1976:
127). Over a series of essays produced across the 1980s that were collected
in *The Rediscovery of the Ordinary* (1991), Njabulo Ndebele later finds
this literature wanting for the manner in which it is saturated with what he
describes as the 'spectacle' (Ndebele [1991] 2006: 31); such a literature, he
will argue, distorts and disempowers its subjects by positioning the state as
the absolute author of the black experience.[1] Interestingly, Ndebele (2006
[1991]: 10, 12) accounts for the prevalence of the 'spectacle' by noting the
absence of a 'compelling ... body of fiction about peasant life'; instead,
'the city appears to have taken tyrannical hold on the imagination of the
average African writer'. He had earlier published a historical analysis of

DOI: 10.4324/9781003174189-4

what he called 'Black Development' (Ndebele 1972) that was attentive to the cleavage between city and country – as well as to the migrant as a figure connecting the two – in *Black Viewpoint*, the journal that Biko edited before he became subject to a banning order. Ndebele was at the time an undergraduate student. Over a decade later, and now as an established author himself, he began publishing essays critiquing what he called the 'literature of commitment' for its numbing 'aesthetics of recognition' (Ndebele 2006 [1991]: 19).

In this reinterpretation of the project of emancipating the mind that Biko had articulated in the slogans quoted above, Ndebele's earlier concern with the occluded countryside remains pronounced in his exaltation of the rural raconteur, even as he acknowledges that the city is the primary domain of black writing. This writing, he argues, would do well to draw on the wellspring of country ways and country aesthetics that bubbles out in the quotidian commutes required of both city-dwellers and labour migrants by the spatial segregation and labour regulations of apartheid. Indeed, Ndebele (2006 [1991]: 25) reports listening to 'countless storytellers' on 'the buses and trains carrying people to and from work' and who he credits with weaving 'masterpieces of entertainment and instruction'. Having thus identified the vehicles of the kind of storytelling that he values, Ndebele (2006 [1991]: 31) formulates the 'rediscovery of the ordinary' as a democratising project that is opposed to the autocratic and exclusionary city ordained by the apartheid regime without being locked into a stance of opposition against it. Critiquing an aesthetic that reduces literature to the act of exposing and confirming an already-defined reality, he finds on the buses and trains connecting countryside, township and city a form of storytelling that elicits 'insights into the social *processes* leading to those finished forms' and which thereby 'involv[e] readers in a truly transforming experience' (Ndebele 2006 [1991]: 15). This kind of storytelling, which travels back and forth between urban and rural spaces, is one in which apartheid is unseated as the author of the black experience even as its subjects are ostensibly being transmitted towards the labour function assigned to them by a system designed to strip them of subjectivity.

The cries of cattle in the kraal

these streets go nowhere
– Mongane Serote, *No Baby Must Weep* (1975)

Protest poetry was launched with the publication of Oswald Mtshali's *Sounds of a Cowhide Drum* (1971). This and subsequent collections by

Mongane Serote, Sipho Sepamla, Mafika Gwala and others expand on the established themes of black urban writing: the lack of rights to the city and the dehumanisation suffered therein. Mtshali's 'Going to Work', for instance, details the quotidian trauma of being reduced to a 'cog' in the 'wheel' of the machine that generates white capital as the speaker, along 'with a thousand black bodies', 'hurtle[s] through stations' toward 'the city skyscrapers'.[2] Sepamla's 'To whom it may concern' in *Hurry Up to It!* (1975) in turn satirises the pernickety discourse of the passbook while observing its power to strip its 'bearer' of identity and to construct him as 'a temporary sojourner' in the city (Sepamla 1975: 40). The register of this poetry, which is often grouped under the epithet 'Soweto' (Chapman 1982), ranges from appeal to bitter irony, and then assertion.

The 'black aesthetic' taking shape in it provoked some condensation and even condemnation, but its proponents responded vigorously to a white-dominated critical establishment, prompting a re-evaluation of the role and reception of literature in repressive states. Gwala's 'In Defense of Poetry' in *No More Lullabies* (1982) questions what is 'poetic' in the shooting of 'defenceless kids' on 'a Soweto street?' For as long as the country 'is unpoetic in its doings', he concludes that 'it'll be poetic to disagree' (Gwala 1982: 10). Denied access to their literary forebears by state censorship and a Bantu Education curriculum that sought to school black subjects for servitude,[3] poets forged new idioms of engagement, often by interweaving their experiences of 'ghetto life' with oral traditions carried over from the countryside as they sought to stimulate 'an awareness of positive values in indigenous culture' (Gwala 1982 [1979]: 169).

The transfusion of rural images and idioms into urban poesis is evident in the title Serote chooses for his inaugural volume, *Yakhal'inkomo* (1972). The author's note explains the allusion:

> Dumile, the sculptor, told me that once in the country he saw a cow being killed. In the kraal cattle were looking on. They were crying for their like, dying at the hands of human beings. Yakhal'inkomo. Dumile held the left side of his chest and said that is where the cry of the cattle hit him … Yakhal'inkomo …
>
> I once saw Mankunku Ngozi blowing his saxophone. Yalkahl'inkomo … He grew tall, shrank, coiled into himself, uncoiled and the cry came out of his horn.
>
> That is the meaning of Yakhal'inkomo.
>
> (Serote 1983 [1972]: iii)

The image of cattle bellowing in the kraal is expressive of a literature that seeks to share the suffering of being black in the city through the act of poetic witnessing (the cry, notably, 'is not that of cattle being slaughtered but of cattle *watching*' [Attwell 2005: 146]).[4] This cry is said to be carried through oral transmission to the city, where it resonates in the brassy 'urban metonym' (Titlestad 2004: 178) of jazz saxophonist Winston Mankunku Ngozi's horn.

Countryside meets city also in the apparently paradoxical imagery with which the poem 'City Johannesburg' opens. Serote here issues his claim by drawing an African 'cultural past and ... cultural presence' (Gwala 1982 [1979]: 170) into the contemporary urban scene as the assured address of the *izibongi* – 'This way I salute you' – counters the anxious gesture of the hand that 'pulses to [his] back trouser pocket' in search of 'my pass, my life'. Nothing, however, seems to evade the maw of this city, which recalls the 'cannibals' of the migrant *sefela*. Each morning it inhales township residents to produce its wealth, exhaling them again each evening: 'That, that is all you need of me' (Serote 1983 [1972]: 13), the speaker bemoans. This city is again shown to be 'Manichean' in structure: Johannesburg is 'life' while townships that are purposefully underdeveloped to contain its labour pool 'are dry like death' (Serote 1983 [1972]: 12, 13). Even when invested with the speaker's 'love', and even as it affirms him and allows him to claim the possessive, the township grants him ownership over little more than 'comic houses ... dongas and ... ever whirling dust' (Serote 1983 [1972]: 12).

When Serote personifies the township as 'mother', he does so in a complex tonal register. In 'Alexandra' (Serote 1983 [1972]: 30–31), he agonises over a landscape of deprivation that has given him the only nurture available.[5] 'Another Alexandra', from his second collection, *Tsetlo* (1974), transfigures this ambiguous mother into a raped woman, her 'dirty petticoat ... soaked in blood' (Serote 1975: 49). The long poem *No Baby Must Weep* (1975), differently, presents the male speaker as wounded, while the mother and/or township tenders a hopeless hope. Refusing any protection that she might offer, he defiantly claims the street as his 'kingdom', albeit one 'ruled by the whistle that tears' through the night, announcing the presence of the police. Thus, he concludes, 'these streets go nowhere'. It is from the apprehension of this dead-end that revolutionary praxis is born. The prescience of this volume, published a year before the Soweto Uprising, is striking.

Hippos in the townships

the street was there all the time, no matter where he was in
Alexandra, to remind him that there had been the days of
Power and the time of the schoolchildren
    – Mongane Serote, *To Every Birth Its Blood* (1981)

43

The student uprising of 16 June 1976 inspired a series of narratives that were produced in white-heat fashion in its wake, including Serote's *To Every Birth Its Blood* (1981), Sepamla's *A Ride on the Whirlwind* (1981), Tlali's *Amandla!* (1980) and Mbulelo Mzamane's *The Children of Soweto* (1982). The demand that the conditions of the time placed on writing to simultaneously mirror, educate and galvanise black urban communities saw a resurgence of prose after the prevalence of poetry in the previous decade. The fiction is at times experimental as the novel form is crafted into a carrier for community mobilisation, rather than serving as the medium of individual experience, and social realism is infused with anticipatory symbolism: suppression is represented while victory is also foretold in this literature that functions simultaneously as record and as a call to arms.

Most plots culminate in political commitment and cross-border flight as they follow the throngs of youth who left the country to join the liberation army with the aim of returning as cadres of the underground struggle. But the narrative action is predominantly located in the townships of Soweto and Alexandra. These settings incite revolt against the deprivation that has been inflicted on them and then nurture this revolt in the nest of community. The township is thus simultaneously synecdoche of apartheid and bedrock of its refusal. Barbara Harlow (1978: 107) notes of Sepamla's Soweto that it 'functions not only as setting, but as an event, idea, and arena of conflict'. So too for the other narratives in which a new vehicle now traffics across the township's dongas: the armoured 'Hippo', and similar trucks such as the 'Casspir' and 'Buffel'. Designed to transport troops into conflict zones – and even to engage in combat themselves – during the apartheid regime's 'border wars' in the independent African states that supported the liberation movement, these armoured vehicles were also deployed in townships as the struggle took root in urban settings. Far from bearing witness to their crushing force, however, the literature commemorates instead the power of the schoolchildren as it seeks to rouse others to join the resistance.

Serote's novel *To Every Birth Its Blood* marks the transition from 'protest' to 'resistance' in particularly stark form, illustrating what Williams (1977) would describe as the shifting 'structure of feeling' in its movement from the alienation and appeal of the first part to the mobilisation of mass action in the second part. As Nick Visser (1987: 425, 428) observes, Serote began the novel 'fully immersed in modernist and existentialist narrative practice', but the eruption of the uprising during its composition 'compelled him to abandon not just one fictional project for another but one kind of novel for another, and one kind of politics for another'. In his later reappraisal, David Attwell (2005: 137, 152, 155) identifies the shift that takes place in Serote's oeuvre (in the poetry as well as this novel) as a movement '[f]rom lyric to epic' – that is, from forms that offered 'a vehicle for expressing selfhood and autonomy' to those that articulate the 'the conjunction between a subject who registers the violence of history on the body, and a developing, communal and more encompassing historical perspective'.[6] 'The quest for epic', he observes, 'begins for Serote in *No Baby Must Weep*', in which 'the focaliser has become unified and more widely representative' (Attwell 2005: 155–156); and it culminates in *Behold Mama, Flowers* (1978), completed during Serote's studies as a Fulbright Scholar in New York and his co-founding of the Medu Art Ensemble in Gaberone, an African National Congress affiliated association for exiled South African and Botswanan 'cultural workers'. *To Every Birth Its Blood*, notes Attwell (2005: 158), 'gives further definition to this moment of choice' in which poetics aligns with politics, its 'structure confirm[ing] the directions already taken in the poetry: Part One tells of the formation of Tsi Molope as a rather dissolute, unfulfilled activist and intellectual; Part Two tells of his absorption into a collective structure'.

The movement *between* the two parts of the novel can be read off the depiction of movements *within* each. Tsi Molope meanders through the first part in a state of detachment; he walks, tellingly, not 'with crowds' but 'into them' (Serote 1981: 5).[7] The *flâneurie* that shapes his narration is shown to be available to him as a man (he wanders from street to street and from woman to woman while the female characters that he visits remain encased in their homes), but it is consistently confined to the township. The 'Golden City' is both prohibitive and traumatising, and the contrast that the narrative draws between it and the 'Dark City' is marked. Though 'a mere nine miles' apart, the white city and the township of Alexandra are presented as antithetical environments, the difference between them being 'like day and night':

> Everything that says anything about the progress of man, the distance which man has made in terms of technology, efficiency and comfort: that Golden City says it well; the Dark City, by contrast, is dirty and deathly. The Golden City belongs to the white people of South Africa, and the Dark City to the black people.
>
> (Serote 1981: 28)

The theme of alienation that runs through the earlier literature is again evoked as Tsi walks through a cemetery, comparing tombstones to 'miniature sky-scapers' (Serote 1981: 10) and observing the corroding carcass of a stolen car before turning back to the 'makeshift place of abode' (Serote 1981: 29) assigned to black city-dwellers. The point of view that he inhabits here is revealing: 'every time I looked at Alexandra from the graveyard, it looked like a graveyard' (Serote 1981: 13). Seeking to maintain an orientation toward life in this gloomy and deprived setting, he urgently catalogues its disparate parts, but they too fail to cohere into a structure that can anchor subjectivity:

> But what is this shit, what is this thing called Alexandra? Seven streets. Twenty-two avenues. Houses. Tin houses. Brick houses. Torn streets. Smell, Dongas. Dirty water in street. Dark city. The devil's kitchen. Township. Alex. What is this mess? Our home. Our country. Our world. Alexandra. Permits. Passes. Police. Security police. Murder and Robbery squad. Paying water accounts. Toilet accounts. House permit. Resident permit. Tax. Rent. Bus fare. Taxi fare. What is Alexandra?
>
> (Serote 1981: 54)

The second part of the novel introduces an abrupt turn from this alienated, individual consciousness posing questions that it is unable to answer. The narrative is now presented through multiple focalisers as Serote depicts a collective of mixed gender laying claim to the city, and to the country at large. The tenor is heroic as activists drive in and out of the central business district, eluding state surveillance and its attempts to demobilise and arrest them. When saboteurs plant a bomb in Johannesburg, the minibus taxi in which they flee back to Alexandra is stopped and searched no less than ten times in the course of a nine-mile journey. Some are caught, but others slip through the dragnet. The struggle of right against might is finally figured in a David-and-Goliath confrontation at a funeral for a slain activist. From a Volkswagen Beetle, activists hurl grenades at a Ford Granada, killing four security police; in retaliation, a herd of armoured Hippos descends upon the funeral, out of which stream 'camouflage uniforms ..., advancing on the mourners, blocking exits, firing teargas' (Serote 1981: 306). One of the comrades who has become known to readers in the preceding pages is captured and falls victim to the torture chamber. Others, along with Tsi Molope, who is now pledged to the struggle, escape 'underground', travelling by rail with returning mineworkers and lying low in rural areas or crossing the border into Botswana.

These closing sequences make subversive use of the carceral figure of a train patrolled by guards who are 'really prison warders' (Serote 1981: 343) in order to connect the urban youth uprising, the movement-in-exile, the migrants who labour in the mine-shafts beneath the city and those who work the soil. The reconnection of city and country in these sequences indicates that the shifting structure of address between the two parts of the novel evidences not only a new commitment to mass action; as Dorothy Driver (1990: 234) notes, it emphasises also that this commitment is founded on a 'return to the world of African communalism' that is understood to be rooted in rural life.

Staffriders and migrants

A mobile, disreputable bearer of tidings
– Mike Kirkwood, 'Staffrider' (1980)

Modes of address continue to turn from the elite and toward the 'everyman' as the literature progressively embeds itself in populist politics through the late 1970s and 1980s. This evolution is further encouraged by the literary magazine *Staffrider* (1978–1993), which elaborates the ways in which the train is redirected to carry the purposeful and collective conclusion to Tsi Molope's story in *To Every Birth Its Blood*.[8] Having previously shifted from ambivalent to negative sign, the train is now reloaded with new content as it picks up the daredevil character of the *tsotsi* culture that had been celebrated during *Drum* magazine's 'fabulous decade'. Hence the title that Mothobi Mutloatse suggested to Mike Kirkwood for the magazine that he founded in 1978. Says Kirkwood (1980: 23): '[h]e explained that a staffrider is some-body who rides "staff" [i.e. not purchasing a ticket] on the fast, dangerous and overcrowded trains that come in from the townships to the city, hanging on the sides of the coaches, climbing on the roof, harassing the passengers'.

In much of the literature surveyed thus far, the motif of travel is deployed to show how the apartheid state relegated black South Africans to the status of the foreign, condemning them to be in perpetual transit through white cities. But the figure of the staffrider re-inserts audacity, agency and asser-tion into this oppressive scene. It does so by refusing to be contained in the carceral carriages of the train even as it still claims the right to go along for the ride, thus accessing the centre on its own terms. The paratextual framing of the magazine's inaugural issue is illustrative of the ways in which black urban life has been constructed by the state as both transitory and confined – and is again expressive of the refusal of this condition that its contents will promote and enact. Photographs by Ralph Ndawo present the constitutive tension between enclosure and traffic that structures black experiences of the colonial-apartheid city: barbed-wire perimeter fencing confines a shad-owy mass of township residents on the front cover; on the back, an intrepid figure leaps clear of this barrier.

Within the magazine's pages, the train carriage itself is also claimed as a space of storytelling. Kirkwood's retrospective account 'Remembering *Staffrider*' observes that '[m]any a *Staffrider* story has begun as … "a thing someone told me on the train"' (Kirkwood 1988: 6). Locomotive imagery, moreover, informs the kinds of writing that the publication fostered and the intervention it sought to make in a segregated literary landscape: emphasising the journey, it published work 'in progress' and established 'lines of communication' between 'writers, their communities, and the general public' ('About Staffrider' 1978: 1).[9] It also drew 'lines of communication' across communities forcibly separated by the state: the South Africa that it projected was one 'in which Meadowlands and Morningside were on the same page, where Douglas Livingstone of Durban and Mango Tshabangu of Jabavu were side by side, with nothing between them but a stretch of paper and a 1-point rule', according to the later recollection of Ivan Vladislavić (2008), who also served a term as editor of the magazine. Chris van Wyk, another *Staffrider* editor, ascribes a similarly connective function to literature in his 'childhood memoir', *Shirley, Goodness and Mercy* (2004). Of the books that propelled him across the borders of the 'coloured' township in which the state would confine him during the 1960s and 1970s, he recalls: 'they take me on journeys to these "Whites Only" places. There's no warning on page 13 or 48 that says: "Stop reading. For 'Whites Only'"' like those signs I've begun to notice at post offices, bus stops, restaurants' (Van Wyk 2004: 68). Later, his reading leads him to Mtshali's *Sounds of a Cowhide Drum*, and thus to the realisation that the black experience of the city can also be the subject of literature; soon his reading list expands to include Nakasa and Abrahams, as well as Paton and Fugard, before he himself emerges among 'the 1976 generation of poets', and then takes his turn as editor of *Staffrider*.

In its inaugural statement, the magazine had notably declined to impose what it presented in scare quotes as '"standards"' and instead advocated 'self-editing' ('About Staffrider' 1978: 1) – a position that aligned it with the Black Consciousness Movement's emphasis on self-reliance. All aspects of *Staffrider*'s production, distribution and reception practices were conceived of as collective and non-profit making. Even after it introduced stronger selection principles and editorial processes, and replaced community contributions with cultural commentary, it still conducted itself as the 'forum' or 'meeting place' announced in its inaugural issue ('About Staffrider' 1978: 1; Van Wyk 1988: 169), thus opening a space in which democratic culture could flourish even in a context of official domination.

The attraction of this space to writers is evident from the content pages of the magazine, which read as a veritable 'who's who' of South African literature at this time. Two notable new voices that were launched in it are those of the short story writers Joël Matlou and Mtutuzeli Matshoba. They fashion, respectively, forms of naïve and documentary realism to sketch subjects drawn taut between motion and stasis, the frenetic and the arrested. Matlou's inaugural 'Man Against Himself' (1979) moves between compound, pass office and train, his protagonist running incessantly through represented space and across the pages of the text in a desperate attempt to stay on track in a segregated and exclusionary city.[10]

The same settings structure Matshoba's prose. 'Call Me Not a Man' (1979) takes as its initial prospect what Kirkwood (1988: 2) describes as 'a typical vantage point in the *Staffrider* landscape, an overhead bridge between station platforms'.[11] From here, the protagonist witnesses police reservists preying on hostel-dwellers while the 'commuter trains coming in from the city ... regurgitate their infinite human cargo' (Matshoba 1979: 19). As is also the case in the story 'To Kill a Man's Pride', trains are shown to strip black urban life down to its labour function. However, Matshoba's stories are also stitched together by these locomotives. He and his fellow passengers subversively inhabit this 'bubble of panoptic and classifying power', to evoke Michel de Certeau's (1984: 11) description of the train, by claiming it as a deliberative public sphere. The vehicle used to disenfranchise Africans from *civitas* thus becomes the very arena in which it is practised and performed.

Matshoba's 'To Kill a Man's Pride' (1980)[12] moves from the train station and the pass office to the dehumanising conditions of the migrant hostels, which are presented simultaneously as synecdoche of the township and its exception. Through a didactic address to a township audience, the story promotes an accord across the townsman–migrant divide that is shown to have opened up so damagingly in works such as *Poppie Nongena*. Valorising rural cultural practices, it suggests that they present an authentic alternative to an urbanity that has been constructed as death to black subjects: '[a]fter an evening of invigorating talk and untainted African traditional song I went away feeling as if I had found treasure in a graveyard' (Matshoba 1980: 123), concludes the narrator. Investigating the city and black life therein, even seemingly functioning as Baudelaire's 'mirror as vast as the crowd itself' (Baudelaire 1964 [1863]: 9), Matshoba's autobiographical protagonist is no *flâneur*: he is participant rather than spectator, and engaged rather than disconnected. The result is what Michael Vaughn (1982: 118) has dubbed a 'popular realism' that takes up the project of consciousness-raising and of advancing black unity in the face of apartheid's divisive strategies through a narrative voice that is both empathetic and edifying.

Agitprop theatre by the *Staffrider* contributors Matsemela Manaka and Maishe Maponya also turns to the migrant predicament to articulate a claim on the city while being less perceptive about its potential. The structuring tropes are by now familiar: in Maponya's *The Hungry Earth* miners are said to be 'eaten' by the city even as it is their 'sweat and bones and blood that made Egoli what it is today' (Maponya 1981:16); and, in Manaka's

Egoli: City of Gold (1978–1982) they are shown digging themselves into a 'living grave' while 'pyramid-like buildings piercing into the sky' (Manaka 1981:15) rise from their labour and their families starve in the reserves. Maponya also uses the motif of the chain to express the characters' literal imprisonment and their symbolic enslavement in the migrant labour system, as well as to expose a pervasive psychic enthrallment to urban modernity. As Bhekizizwe Peterson (1990: 237–238, 249–241) observes, with reference to Gwala (1973), Manaka presents the Black Consciousness Movement's position that 'calling back on the past' is a precondition for 'the forging of the future'; yet, though the play *Egoli* projects a 'utopian vision of pre-colonial African societies' and seeks to demystify the apartheid labour economy, it ultimately presents migrant workers 'as baffled by the politics that regulate their lives' and even feeds into stereotypes of the 'Jim-comes-to-Joburg' variety. Maponya has also been criticised for lack of attention to the experience of women migrants, as well as for his directorial decision to entrust the only female role in *The Hungry Earth*, simply called 'woman' rather than individualised like the other characters, to a male actor due to his belief in the 'unreliability of black women' (Loots 1997).

Mothers of the revolution

> I had intended writing about my own life – the role of women in the struggle. But for reasons I cannot understand, my main character kept dying. In the end I let her, and the story in *Cross of Gold* became a story about the son
> – Lauretta Ngcobo, 'Women Under Pressure' (1991)

The democratic culture that *Staffrider* sought to foster was ultimately male-dominated, even male-centred, and, perhaps surprisingly, it was increasingly so: most of the significant writers of the time published in the magazine, but women's presence therein dwindled noticeably across its lifespan.[13] They were, moreover, excluded from the terms in which it symbolically laid its claim on the city: echoing Biko's formulation – 'Black *man*, you are on your own' – both the titular staffrider and the fugitive scaling the barbed-wire fence on the launch-issue are implicitly gendered male. Matlou and Matshoba also display this emphasis in their short story titles: 'Man Against Himself', 'Call Me Not a Man' and 'To Kill a Man's Pride'; Serote's poetry similarly foregrounds the predicament of the township son or the 'blackmanchild' (Serote 1975) while evoking woman as allegorical mother-figures; and, neither Maponya nor Manaka accommodate women beyond stereotypical appearances.

Ellen Kuzwayo's assertively titled *Call Me Woman* (1985), which offers an apparent rejoinder to Matshoba, addresses this deficiency. Labelled autobiography, it is rather a generically innovative work of nonfiction – as much a history of black women's resistance and a record of Soweto as it is the story of self.[14] Opening with a letter from a woman who had been detained under the Terrorism Act of 1967, Kuzwayo starts with a question: '[w]here is home for a black person in South Africa?' (Kuzwayo 1985: 5). She sets about answering it by detailing the ways in which black women have struggled to claim home-places in a city constructed around the extraction of gold. Her focus is the making of Soweto – first by the state as a monotonous 'dormitory' location intended to house 'the supposedly "temporary" labour force for the ever-growing city of Johannesburg' and then again by the community who make of it what Kuzwayo (1985: 7) defiantly identifies as 'home'. Before relating the personal story of her own 'Road to Soweto' in Part Two, she then proceeds to elaborate the deprivations imposed by the mining industry and the state, and the violent efforts of the latter to suppress the student uprising of 1976. The scene that she depicts is one in which roving 'hippos' render the township a 'battle-field' while the youth retaliate by burning buses and cars in what she describes as a 'terrifying spectacle' (Kuzwayo 1985: 42). Kuzwayo's account of this conflict is, however, by no means tremulous. Performatively enacting the role of 'Mother of Soweto' while aligning herself with the Black Consciousness Movement, she simultaneously claims 'a position of authority over the younger generation' (Driver 1990: 299) and bolsters their struggle by evoking the myriad ways – both quotidian and extraordinary – in which women have refused the assignation of 'temporary sojourners' and 'minors' in the city.

After recording the announcement of Biko's death (which she imagines from the point of view of a parent), and the violent suppression of the outpouring of grief and anger that met it, Kuzwayo ends the first part by seeking a spokesperson against what she presents as a damaging cycle of violence. This she finds in the surprising figure of a woman taxi driver who had helped stem the murders that had come to characterise the industry. Concludes Kuzwayo (1985: 52), before circling back to tell of her own birth: '[t]his is an unusual but significant example of the invaluable contributions made by black women towards the development of their community and country'. The third part of *Call Me Woman* returns to trace 'The Patterns Behind the Struggle'. Notable here is the chapter '"Minors" are Heroines'. The crisis occasioning it is that Kuzwayo must have her son sign her passport application: African women were deemed by the apartheid state to be perpetual minors in law. In response, she recalls the various 'oppressive … barriers' that black women have confronted, starting with the pass laws (Kuzwayo 1985: 241), and proudly notes that women

were successful in their resistance against passes when they were first introduced in 1913 before being finally forced to carry them forty years later.
'Even then', she points out, 'the women did not give in without a struggle'.
Evoking the march of 20,000 women in 1956, she describes the indomitable
attitude with which they arrived from across the country:

> Their resistance was passive; they did not stone anyone or destroy
> anything. They simply sat down in front of the Union Building
> in their thousands and chanted their slogan: 'Strijdom (the prime
> minister at that time) you have met the women, you have struck
> a rock'.
>
> (Kuzwayo 1985: 241)

Until pass laws were finally repealed by the Abolition of Influx Control Act
of 1986, women continued to resist the imposed restriction on their presence in and movements through urban space – often through appeal to their
authority as mothers as well as with analyses of the ways in which pass laws
threatened the fulfilment of their maternal responsibilities (see Gasa 2007).

The impact that the migrant labour system had on mothers is the focus of
Lauretta Ngcobo's novel *And They Didn't Die* (1990), which centres upon
the women consigned to the Bantustans while their husbands labour in the
city. If Kuzwayo is ambivalent in her depiction of rural life (see Driver
1990: 242), Ngcobo's is decidedly unromanticised. She indicts both the racist state and traditional patriarchy in a narrative that revisits the 1960s from
the vantage point of the late 1980s. Elsewhere she comments critically on
how the oral tradition vaunted by the Black Consciousness Movement as a
way of recovering Africa selfhood and self-determination also tutored girls
in self-effacement (Ngcobo 1985: 81). It is a lesson she showed herself to
have learnt only too well when, in her first novel, *Cross of Gold* (1981),
she killed off her revolutionary woman character in the opening chapter.
And They Didn't Die resurrects this woman, as it were. Telling the story of
black women's resistance, it expands their struggle to include the pervasive
threat of starvation in an overcrowded, depleted and now drought-afflicted
reserve; their exposure to white men's sexual violence in urban domestic
labour, in prison when they are jailed for burning their passes and in the
militarised reserve that has been declared their 'homeland'; their casting
as 'vessel' of the patrilineal clan (Ngcobo [1999] 1990: 227); and, being
conscripted to 'produce migrant labour' to service the cities that exclude
them from all but the most precarious domicile (Ngcobo [1999] 1990: 42).

The women in this novel come to recognise that, while they and their
families starve during the drought, they are themselves treated like captive
bodies of water: contained in reservoirs and funnelled through the city in

regulated flows of labour. Under such conditions, both the women and their land lose the ability to support life. The protagonist, Jezile Majola, is thus driven to accept live-in domestic work, which was one of the few legitimate occupations for black women in the apartheid city, in order to remit wages to support her children. In the house of her employer, she discovers the 'abundance' of the white city as 'clean water gushes cold and limitless from the taps', but she is isolated and defenceless when he rapes her in the backyard servant's room. On her return to Sigageni, now bearing the child of rape, Jezile is ostracised by her clan and 'unable to claim for herself her own flesh and blood' (Ngcobo 1999 [1990]: 227). But she does finally make this claim when she saves her daughter from being raped by a soldier in a profound symbolic gesture that locates her resistance in her maternal role (see Samuelson 2012: 765).

As does the story of *Poppie Nongena*, Kuzwayo's and Ngcobo's narratives recast the conditions of the apartheid city through the prism of gender and bring into view the particularly pernicious ways in which black women were positioned by a system that depended on black labour to construct and maintain cities as the preserve of the apartheid state's white citizenry. Both are inevitably shaped by what Ndebele calls the 'spectacle', and they explicitly commemorate women's courageousness in the face of an oppressive and violent state. At the same time, they acknowledge the labour of providing succour – and thus maintaining life itself – in the townships and the Bantustans that had been constructed as dormitories and dumping grounds, thus demonstrating women's tenacity in the quotidian struggle of enduring violence.

Ordinary platforms

[T]he greatest challenge of the South African revolution is in
the search for ways of thinking, ways of perception, that will
help to break down the closed epistemological structures of
South African oppression
    – Njabulo Ndebele, *Rediscovery of the Ordinary* (1991)

In short fiction produced during the 1980s, Ndebele, Tlali and Zoë Wicomb each take up the figure of the train or the act of waiting on the platform to present an aesthetic politics that pushes beyond protest and expands interiority. Variously concerned with rendering 'ordinary' urban lives, opening space for women's voices and enabling critical consciousness, they produce story cycles 'with threaded motifs whose gaps and continuities invite a process of readerly involvement', as Stephen Clingman (2012: 641) notes of Ndebele's collection, and, in the case of Tlali and Wicomb, punctuate their collections with audible silence and audacious speech to communicate gendered subjectivity.

Whereas trains and buses convey the kind of storytelling Ndebele advocates, his critique of 'protest literature' is also carried by this vehicle; it is, he claims,

> a manner of thinking which, over the years, has gathered its own momentum and now reproduces itself uncritically. It is like a train the driver of which has lost control, and it runs dangerously on its fixed rails, passing, with great speed, even where it is supposed to stop.
>
> (Ndebele 2006 [1991]: 55)

Ndebele challenges the ethos of *Staffrider* (to which he was a frequent yet critical contributor) as he calls for pause and reflection, seeking to promote the kind of self-determination and control that he argues would negate apartheid's domination. Instead of staging spectacular conflict, his collection *Fools and Other Stories* (1983) presents the township as the setting of everyday life. The eponymous story opens in the waiting room on a platform in Springs Station on the edge of the East Rand. Rather than referencing alienated labour, the setting provides an occasion for dialogue and contemplation as both travellers embark on a journey toward self-knowledge and social insight: waiting for the train invites interiority or what the story presents as a desire to 'know' the fellow traveller (Ndebele 1983: 152);[15] and, the carriage offers a space of intimacy in which to look him 'in the eyes' (Ndebele 1983: 159), thus becoming the medium through which Ndebele infuses the political with the complex motivations of private life. There is didacticism here, too, but one that seeks to recuperate the resources of the imaginative life, interpersonal interaction and cultural resilience from the perceived impoverishment of protest writing. If the railway line is for Ndebele an emblem of unreflective conformity, then the platform and carriage become in his fiction settings for considered contemplation and exploratory deliberation.

Presenting the township as he does in *Fools*, Ndebele anticipates and even creates the discursive conditions for what Jacob Dlamini – writing from a post-apartheid vantage point – terms 'native nostalgia'. What does it mean, Dlamini asks, for black South Africans to be nostalgic about childhoods spent under apartheid? His response is that it requires conceiving of townships as 'ordinary' spaces in Ndebele's sense. This entails recognising the quotidian practices through which residents neutralised the panopticon structure of the grid-laid townships; not allowing the 'master narrative' to blind one to the 'richness' and 'complexity' of black life under apartheid; viewing townships not as 'zones of deprivation but rather as spaces in which people make 'sense of their worlds' and give 'meaning to their lives'; and, ultimately, appreciating that, while the 'township may have been founded to house Africans who would service white needs', 'it escaped that straitjacket the moment the first brick was laid and the first shack erected' (Dlamini 2009: 43–45, 105, 119, 157).

In another advance toward what Ndebele calls 'the rediscovery of the ordinary', Wicomb's collection *You Can't Get Lost in Cape Town* (1987) articulates the complexity of black life under apartheid through a voice that is forged at – and indeed itself forging – the intersection of Black Consciousness and feminism (Wicomb in Hunter 1993: 88). Whereas Kimberlé Crenshaw introduces the term 'intersectionality' to challenge 'a single-axis framework that erases Black women' with reference to the analogy of a traffic intersection (Crenshaw 1989: 140, 149), Wicomb stages the competing demands of what she refers to as 'the variety of discourses' (Wicomb 2018 [1990]) in apartheid South Africa on a railway platform upon which a girl stands 'uneasily' with her father, awaiting the train to Cape Town beneath the 'black and white arms of the station sign' (Wicomb 1987: 22, 23). She is there by virtue of the fact that her father has exchanged his dream of buying 'a little place ... a little raw brick house and somewhere to tether a goat and keep a few chickens' for an anticipated future in which she 'will drive a white car' (Wicomb 1987: 29, 24); in order to afford her 'the very best education', he will now have to acquiesce to the 'Coloured location' to which they had been moved by state decree and where he is forced to live 'all boxed in with no room to stretch the legs' (Wicomb 1987: 32, 29).

Far from being the kind of instantly recognisable sign of oppression or resistance that Ndebele rues, Frieda's presence on the train platform indicates both privilege and marginality. Her class position as the daughter of the local schoolmaster will transport her to a prestigious convent school in the city that has been opened to 'non-whites', but it is insufficient to keep her family from the 'cramped streets' to which they have been assigned by the Population Registration and Group Areas acts (Wicomb 1987: 29). Her classification as 'Coloured' consigns her to the unpaved section designated for use by 'non-whites', but the policeman 'pacing' the 'white platform' is there 'because of the Blacks' and not for she who averts her gaze from the black girl staggering under the weight of two suitcases while '[h]er madam ambles amiably alongside' (Wicomb 1987: 27, 24). Finally, Frieda's gender subjects her to her father's paternal protection as well as to the scornful surveillance of her male peers, who taunt her with stories of activists 'bury[ing] dynamite between the rails' (Wicomb 1987: 34).

Throughout the cycle of stories, Frieda's narration doubles back ironically on earlier assumptions. As she wavers on the platform that will transport her to the city in 'When the Train Comes', her father rallies her by invoking the alternative fate of servant 'How would you like to peg out the madam's washing and hear the train you once refused to go on rumble by?' he asks, and Frieda pictures herself laundering 'a madam's menstrual rags' (Wicomb 1987: 24). This image is recalled at the end of the eponymous story, when, having deposited her blood-soaked sanitary towel and aborted foetus in the dustbin of an alienating city, she lies waiting for the sound of the morning train. Earlier, finding her way to the backstreet abortion, she struggles to place herself in the city while her white boyfriend exclaims in exasperation that 'you can't get lost in Cape Town' as he points to the picturesque landmarks of mountain and sea. As with the previous translation of images across stories, a later one – 'Home Sweet Home' – returns to denounce the 'postcard beauty of the bay and the majesty of the mountain' from the point of view of the racialised subject that this city would exclude and oppress.

The story 'Home Sweet Home' also troubles the binary of city and countryside that Frieda earlier falls back on as she makes her anxious journey through the streets of Cape Town. En route to the abortion by bus, she had comforted herself with memories of the veld where 'landmarks blaze their permanence' and where 'you can always find your way home' (Wicomb 1987: 73). But 'Home Sweet Home' proves to be as ironically titled as 'You Can't Get Lost in Cape Town': when Frieda walks into the veld she finds that everything has changed, and she is as lost there as she was in the city. It is only in the final story, 'A Trip to the Gifberge', in which she returns from exile in England to visit her now-resurrected mother in rural Namaqualand, that she is able to orient herself by the Southern Cross and find a voice that is not muffled by either her doting father or her white boyfriend. This is a voice anticipated in her disdainful retort, delivered in the Kaaps dialect and rising '[a]bove the noise of a car screeching to a halt' as she 'walks towards the paling' before the mocking eyes of the boys on the platform in 'When the Train Comes': 'Why do you look and kyk gelyk, / Am I miskien of gold gemake?' (lit. 'why do you look and look alike, am I perhaps made of gold?') (Wicomb 1987: 35).

Miriam Tlali's story 'Fud-u-u-a' in her *Footprints in the Quag: Stories and Dialogues from Soweto* (1989) similarly opens a space on the platform 'for the crushed and degraded female to articulate her plight', to quote from Wicomb's (2018 [1990]: 88) own analysis. Tlali's title, the story tells us, is taken from a 'chant sung by distressed commuters trying to get on to crowded trains: they turn their backs to the carriage entrances and wriggle their bottoms in order to make a space for themselves as they chant

"F-u-d-u-u-a!"' (Tlali 1989: 27). The narrative opens with a woman struggling through crowds to reach the station, which is made all the more difficult by the demand of white commuters that blacks 'stick to their "place" by keeping "out of the way"'. A man steadies her as she stumbles toward oncoming traffic, and she thinks 'gratefully': 'Our brothers are usually *so* protective toward us in town here' (Tlali 1989: 28). Racial unity is thus emphasised as a strategy of survival in the apartheid city. But gendered fault lines are observed on the platform, albeit only in a '*whisper*' (Tlali 1989: 33, 41). Tlali herself wriggles, as it were, to make space for her female voice, while a group of black women characters forge a distinct bond to that which is infused by 'the spirit of black solidarity' that muzzles them. *Footprints in the Quag* notably ends with a story titled 'Masechaba's Erring "Child"' about male betrayal being overcome by sisterly solidarity. Men, the collection suggests, transfer traditional practices into urban modernity in selective and self-gratifying ways. Female independence is claimed in Masechaba's concluding resolve to learn how to drive.

Witnessing the interregnum from the suburbs

I live at 6,000 feet in a society whirling, stamping, swaying with the force of revolutionary change ... The city is Johannesburg, the country South Africa, and the time the last years of the colonial era in Africa.
 – Nadine Gordimer, 'Living in the Interregnum' (1988)

While producing its own occlusions, Biko's assertion – 'Black man, you are on your own' – was also a clarion call to white writers to desist from 'speaking for' the oppressed, and to focus instead on examining white consciousness and provoking white conscience. Gordimer's *Burger's Daughter* (1979) absorbs this challenge into its plot as Rosa Burger searches for ways of being relevant in a markedly different era to that of the Defiance Campaign (1951–1953) and the Rivonia Trial (1963–1964) in which her father had played significant roles, and which sustained the tentative extension of friendship that concludes *A World of Strangers*.[16] André Brink's *A Dry White Season* (1979),[17] in turn, responds to the challenge of Black Consciousness with a story of state exposure and white witnessing. Whereas Gordimer leans towards modernism to situate 'commitment' within 'the whole ontological problem in life' (Gordimer & Ross 1987: 140), Brink draws on documentary realism and the spy thriller genre to craft a narrative that demonstrates 'responsibility towards truth' (Brink in Kossew 1996: 26).

Readers are told at the outset of Brink's generic hybrid that the death of Ben du Toit, which had been officially recorded as a hit-and-run accident, was an assassination. What remains to be uncovered is the route by which he has strayed from the security of the white suburbs into the belly of the beast, as well the nature of the beast itself. As is also the case with Ben's death, this enquiry is carried by automobile: that of the taxi driver Stanley Makhaya who transports him into the townships. Says Ben, after his first conveyance to what he had previously considered 'the dark side of the moon': 'I had to see it with my own eyes. Now I know' (Brink 2011 [1979]: 96). The purpose of the narrative is said to be so that no white South African can again say, '*I knew nothing about it*' (Brink 2011 [1979]: 237). Taking its title and epigraph from Serote's poem 'For Don M. – Banned',[18] which consoles its addressee in an oppressive state with an awareness of the organic cycles of time ('it is a dry white season … but seasons come to pass'), Brink's novel maintains an optimism toward the future. Gordimer's *July's People* (1981), which adopts a speculative mode, is more hesitant. Gordimer uses as epigraph the bleak statement from Antonio Gramsci's *Prison Notebooks*: '[t]he old is dying and the new cannot be born; in this interregnum there arises a great diversity of morbid symptoms'. Whereas Coetzee (1988: 11) defines an earlier body of 'white writing' that was preoccupied with the land as being generated by 'a people no longer European, not yet African', this writing by whites in the interregnum might be described as uneasily poised between a rejection of the colonial-apartheid city and trepidation before an uncertain urban future.

July's People casts toward this future, but then equivocates on the threshold. The plot concerns the flight of a white family from the suburbs as an army of black revolutionaries march from Soweto to occupy the city. Under the protection of their house-servant, July, they are taken to his family in the rural village, to which the white state had confined them while drawing on July's urban labour. Past power relations are awkwardly reversed, but white dependency remains consistent in this dumping-ground turned sanctuary. The conclusion is 'open yet arrested', and emblematic of a writing 'end-stopped' before the future (Boehmer 1998: 48, 50): the stranded suburban housewife runs towards a helicopter, not knowing whether it bears 'saviours or murderers', but simply fleeing her situation as 'the enemy of all that would make claims of responsibility' (Gordimer 1982 [1981]: 158, 159).

The city is again the battleground for an undetermined future in Coetzee's *Life & Times of Michael K* (1983). Eluding curfew patrols, Michael K wheels his sick mother out of Cape Town in a barrow and, after she dies, he attempts 'living off the land' by becoming a 'cultivator' (Coetzee 1985 [1983]: 46, 59) on an abandoned farm. Coetzee, however, shuns a narrative trajectory that would present 'a justification of pastoralism' (Attwell, 2015:

145). Michael K is caught and sent to a work camp servicing the neighbouring farms, his imposed rural servitude analogous to the urban situation in which his mother laboured as a live-in domestic while being accommodated in a maintenance room beneath the stairs of the apartment that she cleaned: tucked out of sight, the camp residents 'come on tiptoe in the middle of the night like fairies and do their work, dig their gardens, wash their pots, and be gone in the morning leaving everything nice and clean' (Coetzee 1985 [1983]: 82).

After fleeing the work camp and being recaptured once more, Michael K is interned in a 'rehabilitation' camp in Cape Town in order to be made well again so that 'he can rejoin camp life and have a chance to march back and forth across the racetrack and shout slogans and salute the flag and practice digging holes and filling them again' (Coetzee 1985 [1983]: 133); it is a fate prefigured in the 'travelling incarceration' of the train (De Certeau 1984: 111) that links these various camps and the places that they service: '"Why does it matter where they are taking us? ... There are only two places, up the line and down the line. That is the nature of trains"' (Coetzee 1985 [1983]: 41). While recalling the image of the township-as-prison in *Poppie Nongena*, Coetzee's vision of the city-as-camp is prescient of the late apartheid state and, indeed, of its aftermath. Responding with typical belligerence to the resistance movement's strategy of rendering the townships 'ungovernable', PW Botha's government declared a State of Emergency in 1985 that was ultimately extended until 1989.[19] 'The camp', notes Georgio Agamben (2005: 168–169), 'is the space that is opened when the state of exception begins to become the rule'. Coetzee's Michael K – the consummate 'escape artist' who evades even the spatiotemporal fixity of 'committed writing' – points readers to the ubiquity and persistence of the urban formations that took shape in a repressive state: in a vision that writers will return to after the formal end of apartheid, the city is itself shown to become a 'fortress', its 'high walls' detaching from the time of war and marching into a future in which they will construct new enclosures (Coetzee 1985 [1983]: 160, 147).

Coetzee returns to recognisable coordinates of time and space in *Age of Iron* (1990) only to mark their disturbance in the interregnum. Embarking on a revelatory quest, Mrs Curren – a retired and terminally ill Professor of Classics – drives from the suburbs of Cape Town to the conflagrating townships in search of her domestic worker's son. The setting that she enters is that of the KTC and Crossroads informal settlements, where a state-sponsored black vigilante group identified by the white arm- and headbands that they sported (hence the moniker '*witdoeke*'; lit. 'white cloths') destroyed over 60,000 dwellings during an assault enacted through the months of May and June 1986 that was part of an extended war waged against militant township youth (*Poppie Nongena* represents an earlier phase in this conflict). Derek Attridge (2012: 177) observes that the scene in which Mrs Curren enters this setting 'attempt[s] to convey the horror of the violence rending the townships and settlements in the traumatic year of 1986 with a directness that brings Coetzee closer to historical reportage than anywhere else in his fiction'. The emphasis placed on the perspective through which it is filtered ensures, however, that readers are 'not allowed to forget that *Age of Iron*'s pages on township violence are the representation, first, of a (fictional) middle-class white woman who has benefitted from an extensive education and, secondly, of a (real) middle-class white man who has similarly benefitted' (Attridge 2012: 183). Readers are thus encouraged 'to examine [this representation] for its limitations and biases', including the ways in which Mrs Curren casts the 'scenes of horror and misery' that she witnesses 'through the lens of her classical and post-classical reading' (Attridge 2012: 183, 185). Received through this lens, the journey that she undertakes is depicted as one from the state-directed oblivion of the suburbs into a disorienting and nightmarish Virgilian underworld. (There are echoes here also of 'Coda' to *In This City* (1986) by Stephen Watson [1986: 34], published in the year in which *Age of Iron* is set, in which the 'city on a peninsula, between the mountain and the sea' with its 'great dualities, divided peoples', is said to have delivered 'early on, over and over, a very clear idea of hell.')

Through Mrs Curren, Coetzee asks questions about the representational politics of the white writer who seeks the words to denounce the location of hell at the edge of a picturesque city. Taking in the view of False Bay, she marks her distance from the poetics of protest and what Louise Bethlehem (2001) has described as its 'rhetoric of urgency': 'A sense of urgency is what keeps deserting me. Sitting here among all this beauty, or even sitting at home among my own things, it seems hardly possible to believe there is a zone of killing and degradation all around me' (Coetzee 1990). Tropes from earlier white writing return for re-evaluation: the discarded subjects of Fugard's drama – '[w]e shoot these people as if they are waste, but in the end it is we whose lives are not worth living' (Coetzee 1990); Burgess's boarding-house subjects claiming the racialised spoils of the city – '[i]n the exhausted car the two of us must have looked like nothing so much as belated refugees from the *platteland* [lit. 'flat land'; countryside] of the Great Depression' (Coetzee 1990); and, the re-surfacing corpse that indicates the irrepressible black claim on the land in Gordimer's *The Conservationist* (1974) but which here portends a more ominous future:

> when I walk on this land, this South Africa, I have a gathering feeling of walking upon black faces. They are dead but their spirit has not left them. They lie there heavy and obdurate, waiting for my

feet to pass, waiting for me to go, waiting to be raised up ... The
age of iron waiting to return.

(Coetzee 1990)

A decade earlier, Serote had concluded his novel of urban insurrection with
the hopeful image of a woman giving birth. These novels of the interregnum
suggest instead the failure of the new to emerge as they anticipate the ways
in which old structures may persist in a future embodied by children who
have been brutalised by the state and cast into the wretched peripheries of
its 'Manichean' cities.

Notes

1 The argument is made over a series of essays and addresses between 1984 and
   1987, and later published as *The Rediscovery of the Ordinary: Essays on South
   African Literature and Culture* (1991).
2 For discussion of other allusions to trains in this poetry, see Jones (2018).
3 Writers of the 1970s were denied the foundations dug by earlier generations.
   Mzamane and Sepamla recall the 1950s as 'our cultural golden age' but note
   that, 'came Sharpeville and the law descended on us with its heavy boot. In
   1963 the Publications Law lopped off our heads with one fell swoop ...
   Overnight Mphahlele's *Down Second Avenue*; Rive's *Emergency*; Matshikiza's
   Chocolates for My Wife and other works disappeared as if from the face of the
   earth' (Sepamla 1980: 25).
4 In *Muriel at Metropolitan*, a character similarly interpolates the bellow of the
   slaughtered beast into the urban setting of the hire-purchase store to express his
   unease with luring customers to buy on credit while knowing their purchases
   may soon be subject to repossession: 'It makes me feel guilty, like I've brought
   him to be slaughtered' (Tlali 1979: 17).
5 Alexandra was first established in 1912 as a freehold township, sharing this
   much-prized status with Sophiatown. Situated near the wealthy suburb of
   Sandton, Alexandra was poorly resourced, allowing for a study in the contrasts
   that have characterised the apartheid city. Along with the 'Soweto Uprising'
   of 1976, which quickly travelled Alexandra, it has been the site of sustained
   resistance against the segregating city, including bus boycotts through the 1940s
   and 1950s that protested increased fares on the labour commute, and resistance
   through the 1960s and 1970s against the state's attempt to transform it into a
   'hostel city' comprised entirely of labour barracks. For further background, see
   Bonner and Nieftagodien, *Alexandra: A History* (2008).
6 Attwell (2005: 137) quotes from Jeremy Cronin's *Even the Dead* (1997) –
   'Between, let's say, May 1984 and May 1986 ... / There was a shift out there /
   From lyric to epic' – 'but moves the dates back by a decade'.
7 There are echoes of the protagonist in La Guma's debut, *A Walk in the Night*
   (1962), and a somewhat similar shift to that observed within Serote's novel can
   be traced across La Guma's oeuvre.
8 More short-lived literary magazines published between the '*Drum* decade' and
   the emergence of *Staffrider*, or during the longer lifespan of the latter, include:
   Purple Renoster (edited Lionel Abrahams, 1956–1972), *The Classic* (edited first

by Nat Nasaka and then Barney Simon, 1963–1971), *New Classic* (1975–1978) and *The Classic* (1980–1982) edited Sepamla, and his earlier *S'Ketsch* (1972–1975) (see Kruger 2013: 104).

9　The mission statement 'About Staffrider' (1978) appears to have been written by Kirkwood, but deliberately avoids being ascribed to an editor: 'The magazine is being prepared for publication by RAVAN Press but has no editor or editorial board in the usual sense'.

10　Later published as part of Matlou's collection *Life at Home, and Other Stories* (Johannesburg, COSAW: 1991).

11　Published also as the titular story of Matshoba's collection *Call Me Not a Man* (1979), which was the second volume of Ravan Press's 'Staffrider Series'.

12　Republished in Motloatse's compilation *Forced Landing* (1980), the third volume of the 'Staffrider Series'.

13　From a tentative beginning in which women comprised nearly a fifth of contributors, they had by the end of the magazine's life been reduced to a mere 10% (see Mofokeng 1989; Gqola 2001).

14　For further discussion of the generic innovation of *Call Me Woman*, see Driver (1990) and other sources discussed in Samuelson (2012).

15　The first paragraph of the story opens and closes as follows: 'When I first saw him in the waiting room on platform one at Springs Station, I wanted to know him … I wondered who he was, and where he came from' (Ndebele 1983: 152).

16　See Clingman, who asserts that the Black Consciousness Movement was 'the primary phenomenon to which *Burger's Daughter* responded' (Clingman 1986: 170); the father, Lionel Burger, is in part modelled on the communist anti-apartheid activist and lawyer Bram Fischer, who led the defence at the Rivonia Trial (1963–1964) and was later himself sentenced to life imprisonment.

17　Rather than a translated text in the conventional sense, both English and Afrikaans versions of the novel were written by Brink.

18　Don Mattera, author of the Sophiatown memoir *Memory Is the Weapon*, who was under banning orders from 1973 to 1982.

19　The 1985 State of Emergency initially applied to 36 magisterial districts in the Eastern Cape and the Pretoria-Witwatersrand-Vaal (the PWV area that would become Gauteng after 1994) and later extended to include the Western Cape; by mid-1986 its reach was nation-wide and in 1987 it was renewed for a further two years. Though not exclusively urban, it was particularly so, and characterised by the deployment of armed troops in townships, among other repressive measures.

5

REASSEMBLING THE CITY

The child is not dead
Not at Langa nor at Nyanga
nor at Orlando nor at Sharpeville
nor at the police post at Philippi
where he lies with a bullet through his brain ...

the child is present at all assemblies and law-giving ...

the child grown to a man treks on through all Africa
the child grown to a giant journeys
over the whole world
without a pass!
                    – Nelson Mandela's rendition of 'Die Kind'
                           by Ingrid Jonker (Mandela 1994b)

During his first State of the Nation address on 24 May 1994, Nelson Mandela presented the translation of Ingrid Jonker's poem 'Die Kind' ('The Child') that is excerpted in the epigraph.[1] Drawn between searing indictment and specu-lative hope, 'Die Kind' had been penned by Jonker in a furious response to the state's massacre of anti-pass protestors in Sharpeville and Nyanga in 1960. Recontextualised through Mandela's iteration, it conveyed the message that the country was now entering the unrestricted state that Jonker had earlier forecast, and which had been realised through the liberation struggle that had grown out of the anti-pass protests. Presented in the Houses of Parliament by the first democratically elected President of South Africa, this rehearsal of the poem ten-dered an optimistic figure of the redoubtable spirit claiming mobility as its right and reassembling the fractured forms of the colonial-apartheid city into a new polity. The inclusive gesture of citing a poet who was 'both an Afrikaner and an African' (Mandela 1994b) contributed also to the aura of the South African 'miracle' that illuminated the transition.

Although the euphoria of the moment soon faded, some of the spirit of defiance and expectancy that informs the poem, as well as the occasion of

DOI: 10.4324/9781003174189-5

63

its recitation, endures in the writing of the city through the following two decades. Much of the literature produced during this period is preoccupied with tracking the persistence of 'morbid' structures into the post-apartheid city and with registering the duplicity of the dreams that have been invested in it. But, while contending with the ways in which the colonial-apartheid city has morphed into an assemblage of 'camps' or exclusionary citadels that abject the multitudes 'The Child' would accommodate, some continue to seek forms through which to activate the polis of assembly and to reimagine the city as a place of community and even of care.

City of dreams; or city of death and dis-ease

a place where dreams come to die
– Perfect Hlongwane, *Jozi* (2013)

Many writers revisit and replot migrant narratives as they grapple with the question of whether the 'city of dreams' towards which Mandela directed his youthful self in the early chapters of his 'long walk to freedom' has finally been achieved. Most respond to this question in the negative, or at best ambiguously. Some reprise the trope of the contaminating or cannibalistic city to show how persistent – if revised – conditions of precarity undermine post-apartheid aspirations. Others elaborate a new thematic constellation in which dreams dissolve into delusions as psychotic and drug-fuelled hallucinations frame visions of the city as a chimera. The pathologies of HIV/ AIDS, bipolar disorder and schizophrenia are used to indicate the dis-ease of those inhabiting this city, and many succumb also to violent crime or self-annihilation.

Not all is bleak and gloomy, though. The chronic and terminal nature of the maladies through which the city is rendered may preclude happy endings – and many narratives do indeed conclude in despair – but much of the literature also looks to assuage the eviscerating effects of alienation as it maintains an orientation – sometimes stoic, sometimes wistful – towards the city as a site in which a new national subject might be assembled. As writers continue to strive for what Simone (2004) calls 'the city yet to come', they make increasing use of speculative and fantastical forms. Prevalent also are genres that convey a chiaroscuro effect, such as tragicomedy and noir fantasy, as well as a graphic naturalism that ruptures its grim determinations with vivid hallucinatory sequences or startling expressions of tenderness.

Marlene van Niekerk's dark comedy *Triomf* (1994; trans. 1999) is set on the eve of the 1994 elections.[2] Recalling how the National Party won support for apartheid through 'poor white' upliftment policies that claimed the city for indigent Afrikaners by evicting other communities and erasing their urban worlds, the novel reveals how dystopia is simultaneously the ideal society gone wrong and its constitutive outside.[3] Triomf ('triumph') is the name of the 'whites only' suburb that was built on the ruins of Sophiatown, and the characters' backstory shows how it was made available to Afrikaners who had migrated to the city after the Great Depression reduced them to destitute tenant farmers. Throughout the narrative, rubble surfaces as a reminder of the destruction that this crowing 'city of dreams' had visited upon another. The construction on this pilfered terrain is, moreover, a place of chaotic derangement as the white city is shown to be enervating even to those for whom it was intended: the line of this incestuous family has entered a 'cul-de-sac' and is likened also to a 'bulldozer in a sinkhole' (Van Niekerk 1999 [1994]: 65). The symbolism is developed in a conclusion in which the already-enfeebled patriarch is inadvertently killed when the house is whitewashed during a farcical scene of home improvement.

Also darkly comic in its address to a transitional present is Zakes Mda's *Ways of Dying* (1995). Mda reprises the story of migration from the rural village to the late apartheid city as an 'odyssey' for 'love and fortune' while at the same time presenting the violence and deprivation of an informal settlement that became one of the battlegrounds in the struggle for the city during the 1970s and 1980s (it is the place represented as prison and as hell in Joubert's *Poppie Nongena* and by Coetzee's Mrs Curren). Featuring a carnivalesque character who fashions an eccentric role for himself as a 'professional mourner', *Ways of Dying* sustains an ebullient mood even as it is plotted around the ubiquity of death. This mood is enabled by the maintenance of a formal connection to the countryside: the story is narrated in the 'communal voice' of village gossip and is fabulous in its composition. Yet, instead of counselling flight, as an earlier literature of migration to the city-of-death might have done, *Ways of Dying* refigures the meanings of urban morbidity: characters perform the work of mourning in order to issue their claim on the city rather than in retreat from it as they do in Paton's *Cry, the Beloved Country*; and, pervasive mortality is shown to produce a choral cacophony in a cemetery that represents not just the consuming nature of the city but also its invigorating clamour.

The claim on the city that is expressed in *Ways of Dying* is altogether an assured one. What the apartheid state sought to retain as *informal* settlements in order to eradicate them easier are shown taking root and sprouting schools and shops, while informal trading practices travel into the central business district, where they establish a parallel economy to the malls that they abut. Rather than hankering after a different kind of city and remaining attached to the devouring dreams of the glittering metropolis, *Ways of Dying* embraces the forms of cityness that have evolved across the continent – and around the global south – in which 'informality is the norm' and practices of 'making do' are best understood not as aberration but rather as the means by which the claim on the city is sustained and by which 'individuals or groups try out or invent new social or economic roles in an attempt to make the city work for themselves' (Pieterse 2011: 14; Bremner 2002: 166). In his self-appointed role as 'professional mourner', the novel's peculiar protagonist is shown traversing the city, adamant in his assertion that he has 'all the right in the world' to do so (Mda 1995: 22). His 'peripatetic' wanderings render it in turn a 'dynamic entity', as Rita Barnard (2007: 152) has observed. This lively recasting of urban space marks a notable movement out of the imprisoning location of apartheid cartography that confined Serote's protagonist to the boundaries of Alexandra in the first part of *To Every Birth Its Blood* and which is in some literature of that period identified with the incarcerating carriages of the train.

But Mda also accurately predicts the resilience of the shantytown, which, through the subsequent decades, has continued to mushroom into the margins that apartheid's city planners drew between the white suburbs and black townships. Rather than anticipating the accommodation of squatters by the city – apparently too large a leap for even a novel that draws readily on magical realist devices – *Ways of Dying* offers a cheerful but superficial panacea: redecorating a shack with pages from discarded copies of the glossy *Garden & Home* magazine that afford its inhabitants imaginative passage into suburban life. The trope of debris is multivalent: it indicates that the claim on the city continues to be reduced to the recycling of rubbish that had evacuated earlier characters such as Fugard's Boesman and Lena and which mirrored their own status as the jettisoned subjects of the city; at the same time, as in *Triomf*, it is suggestive of how multiple, and often conflicting, urban dreams jostle in a transitional present that seeks to give form to the emergent city.

The question of form is central to Ivan Vladislavić's *The Restless Supermarket* (2001), which 'exposes the fantasy of a post-apartheid utopia' through a postmodern parody of urban management in a city pulled between vertiginous change and anxious conservation (Robinson 2010: 234). The farcical narrator is Aubrey Tearle, a retired proofreader who rues declining linguistic standards and recoils from the transformation of the erstwhile white suburb of Hillbrow into what Nuttall (2008: 205), in her reading of the novel, parses as a 'diverse, disorderly Afropolitan inner-city quarter'. Aubrey Tearle seeks refuge from what he perceives as the encroaching chaos in his beloved Café Europa. This last outpost of what he identifies as the ideal city – both orderly and uniform – is itself adorned with the image of an urban utopia, in this case a painting of the imaginary city of 'Alibia'. Referencing whiteness while offering Tearle the vista of 'a generous elsewhere' (Vladislavić 2001: 19), Alibia presents the hysterical enactment of metropolitan mimicry that typifies the 'racial city' (see Mbembe 2008: 38–39, 62).

The second part of the novel takes the form of a metafictional fantasy in which a Society of Proofreaders move about the city, deleting and correcting, sorting the 'cacophony of categories' and endeavouring 'to preserve the proper boundaries between things' (Vladislavić 2001: 189, 209). The forces of chaos seem to be ascendant as a shop flies off and a shantytown falls into the space it has vacated, but the Proofreaders are ultimately victorious in restoring order. Not so for the external reality to which Aubrey Tearle returns in the final part, however: the Goodbye Bash in Café Europa collapses into a muddle from which this curmudgeonly witness to change is unable to hold himself aloof, and he is left with the realisation that he has unwittingly unleashed upon the world a document 'riddled with corrigenda' (Vladislavić 2001: 303).

While humorously mocking the agitation of an anachronistic white character in the face of a shifting city, the novel is also critiquing what Vladislavić will bemoan in his later work, *Double Negative* (2011: 12), as the 'age of the mall' or the imposition of an urban structure that proliferates parking lots and rides roughshod over neighbourhood sociality. The historical movement that *The Restless Supermarket* registers is also part of the strategic retreat of capital from the central business district of Johannesburg and into the northern suburbs as those who had been previously excluded from it claimed the right to inhabit the centre; thus decentralised, the retail function 'has increasingly aggregated in suburban shopping malls' (Titlestad 2012: 677). Torn between heralding de-racialisation and ruing the reorganisation of urban life around the standardised consumption practices peddled in the city-as-supermarket, the tone of Vladiskavić's novel is as often bittersweet as it is satirical. While showing up the intractable prejudices that have sought to fend off the post-apartheid city, the narrative hall of mirrors is at the same time reflective of an authorial concern with the manner in which South African cities are being reconfigured in the 'movement from a European model of what a city is' – the model to which Aubrey Tearle subscribes – 'to an American model' (Vladislavić in Miller 2011 [2006]).

Hillbrow – the inner-city area of Johannesburg in which Vladislavić's 'aging white man' (Nuttall 2008: 204) finds himself increasingly discomposed – has witnessed some of the most striking demographic shifts in urban South Africa. Once the racially exclusive suburb inhabited by the 'pass-for-white' brother of Essop's Hajji, it transformed through the late 1980s into what was termed a 'grey area' as the grip of the Group Areas Act was gradually loosened over certain quarters. The capacity for rapid change that this area of Johannesburg has demonstrated (see Mpe 2003: 184–185) is celebrated in Phaswane Mpe's *Welcome to Our Hillbrow* (2001). Succeeding the transformations that Aubrey Tearle witnessed, Mpe's narrative can be seen to present the next chapter in Hillbrow's story – one in which it comes to house African immigrants drawn to the prospects of the liberated state of Mandela's South Africa, along with students of the nearby University of the Witwatersrand. Now the country's most densely populated area, Hillbrow is famous for the teeming street life that Mpe's novel conveys through breathlessly long sentences, and notorious for a crime rate that is in part registered in its post-mortem, second person narrative voice.

Mpe's rural villagers denounce the city through the folkloric figure of the 'swallowing monster', and their prejudice appears to be borne out by the fact that all the major characters do indeed die. The narrative does, however, part ways with the 'Jim comes to Joburg' arc that would deny or deride African claims on the city. The moral dichotomy that its terminal plots might be seen to confirm is scrupulously subverted: far from being the kinds of antitheses that structure *An African Tragedy* or *Cry, the Beloved Country*, urban Hillbrow and rural Tiragalong are each shown suffer their own 'moral decay' (Mpe 2001: 17). Traversed as they are by itinerant characters, the two spaces infuse one another rather than holding apart; as the narrator puts it: 'Tiragalong was in Hillbrow. You always took Tiragalong with you in your consciousness whenever you came to Hillbrow or any other place. In the same way, you carried Hillbrow with you always' (Mpe 2001: 49). Whereas the colonial-apartheid state sought to drive a wedge between city and countryside, Mpe interlinks and enfolds the two through narrative recursion, shifting perspectives and the trajectories of his characters, which together connect Hillbrow 'to a South African and African hinterland' (Titlestad 2012: 682). In the process, he forges what Neville Hoad defines as an 'African cosmopolitanism' (Hoad 2006). This is an attitude and way of being in the world that maintains an unwavering urban orientation while attaching also to other spaces, whether in rural South Africa or across the continent and the world-at-large, and which reaches ultimately even into the cosmic sphere.

Mpe's contemporary, K. Sello Duiker, makes a similar claim on and from the post-apartheid city.[4] Duiker draws inspiration from southern African precursors such as Bessie Head and Dambudzo Marechera as he depicts the gritty underside of Cape Town while piercing it with prodigious visions. The effect is not exactly magical realist, although Ben Okri is also clearly an influence; rather than revealing the collision of different worlds, Duiker conjures the cracks into which certain subjects fall and from which luminous ways of seeing might yet also shimmer forth.

In an essay titled 'The Streets and the Gods of Truth', Duiker writes of how he became aware of an 'ignored member of street life' amidst 'the bustle' of the city (Duiker 2004: 9). Whereas he remembers the township culture of his youth as being both vivifying and traumatising, the children living on the city streets are, unequivocally, 'at the complete mercy of its darkness' (Duiker 2004: 9). His first novel, *Thirteen Cents* (2000), 'is about their long nights' (Duiker 2004: 9). Narrated in the present tense by one such child, Azure, *Thirteen Cents* gives readers intimate and immediate access to his street-level perspective. Various cities come into view and overlap as Azure moves across an 'uneven' geography in which the chasms that were bored out and policed under apartheid now advance the progress of the neoliberal state (Harvey 2005: 87). 'The freedoms [that such a state] embodies', notes David Harvey (2005: 7), 'reflect the interests of private property owners, businesses, multinational corporations, and financial capital'. Azure's itineraries expose also what Jean and John Comaroff (2006: 6) describe as the '*pas de deux*' of licit and illicit economies that characterises the neoliberal state in the postcolony. As he traverses the city pervaded by finance capitalism, administered by investment bankers and consumed by the global elite, as well as that which is ruled by gangsters and pimps, it becomes clear that these cities are two sides of the same coin, and that the function of this coin is to commodify life itself.

Thirteen Cents seems initially to be a *Bildungsroman*, but the genre is inadequate to Azure's experiences in a city in which maturity is both denied and prematurely pressed upon him. Exploited and betrayed by all potential instructor figures, he has to 'Grow up. Fast. Very fast. Lightning speed' (Duiker 2000: 66). At thirteen years, he declares that he is 'not a boy', having witnessed and experienced too much abuse for his age: 'A boy? Fuck off … I have seen enough rubbish to fill the sea. I have been fucked by enough bastards and they've come on me with enough come to fill the swimming pool in Sea Point' (Duiker 2000: 142). Rather than an unfurling into adulthood, his is a life measured in a handful of small change. Instead of arriving at an accommodation with the society in which he has been exploited, Azure flees it and ascends the mountain. It is a significant destination: slaves escaping the colonial town sought refuge on Table Mountain, and Duiker associates it also with the indigenous peoples who were displaced from their ancestral hunting grounds and pasturage on its slopes in a genocidal annihilation that cleared the ground for the waystation on the East India trade route that was later claimed as the 'mother city' of white South Africa.[5] While taking refuge in a cave, Azure dreams also of the woman Saartjie Baartman, who was exhibited and dissected as the 'Hottentot Venus' in imperial London and Paris in the early nineteenth century. Like these antecedents, he too has been subsumed in and seeks an exit from the metropolitan 'money economy'.

Entering into shamanistic trances on the mountain, Azure appears to awaken primordial forces that would avenge his abuse. He watches from the summit as T-Rex metes out one such punishment, 'stomping over cars and tearing apart buildings ... destroying the city' (Duiker 2000: 121). This and subsequent scenes of retribution exacted by natural forces on the built environment may be received as a challenge to a city that continues to commodify and consume life in an apparently new dispensation that has merely refurbished its colonial-apartheid structures to serve the interests of capital accumulation. At the same time, these scenes offer an early expression of the Anthropocene epoch that was first proposed in the year in which *Thirteen Cents* was published, and which identifies 'the human' as a geological force disrupting the earth system to such an extent that the survival of the species along with myriad other life forms may be threatened (Crutzen & Stoermer 2000). Recalling the extinction event of 66 million years ago that abruptly concluded the Cretaceous Period and the Mesozoic Era, the T-Rex that is shown rampaging through the city in *Thirteen Cents* is both agent and object of destruction. Roused from its slumbers in deep history, it rips through the concrete structures of late capitalism that are rendering the planet itself as unhabitable as the city that denies Azure both security and sustenance.

Shortly after T-Rex's rampage, Azure observes how the sea appears as a 'blue plastic thing that ... moves gently like a conveyor belt' (Duiker 2000: 132). Its elemental power is thus seen to have been tamed into a frictionless, petrochemical-produced surface over which capital – encrypted in an endless procession of container ships – flows in and out of the port city and around a planet that has been reduced to a factory for finance. But, as anticipated in various climate change scenarios, the deranged earth system bites back: Azure watches the ocean 'coming alive' (Duiker 2000: 160) until it engulfs the town in the novel's concluding scene. The trope recurs in Kelwyn Sole's poem 'Cape Town™' (Sole 2010) when the speaker turns in repugnance from a city in which 'money holds' its residents 'in thrall, a lock that never rusts', and imagines an 'enormous wave upwelling' to loosen it from the stays of lucre and set it afloat in a 'continent' 'of water' in which 'everything is gloriously not in order'. But the apocalyptic conclusion to *Thirteen Cents* suggests more the impossibility of becoming for Azure than a resolution to his plight: although there may be satisfaction for readers in the punishment meted out on the town in the closing sequence, he himself is left fearful and grieving.

Alert to the disparities in the consumption of goods that the species term 'Anthropos' would obscure, *Thirteen Cents* is thus also expressive of the inequitable distribution of vulnerability to the harms that it has unleashed.[6] What it points to is the complex that Jason Moore has dubbed the 'Capitalocene' – a term which names the 'climate crisis' as 'a geohistorical moment that systemically combines greenhouse gas pollution with the climate class divide, class patriarchy, and climate apartheid' (Moore 2019: 54). Constructed through the extraction of what Moore calls 'Cheap Nature' and providing the template for global 'climate apartheid' (Moore 2019: 54) in its production of cheap labour,[7] the South African city is one exemplary site for studying the Capitalocene.[8]

Duiker's subsequent novel, *The Quiet Violence of Dreams* (2001), in turn, questions the notion of democratisation being achieved through expanded consumption. Seeking to get 'beneath the skin of Cape Town's postcard beauty', the narrative roves across the city's fragmented surface (Duiker in Van der Merwe 2005). The range of 'morbid symptoms' exhibited in it suggest entrapment in an interminable interregnum: the protagonist, Tshepo, suffers psychosis, is raped and, after finding temporary sanctuary in a male massage parlour, is advertised therein in dehumanising and racist terms as the 'black stallion' (Duiker 2001: 271). Initially seduced by the glittering surfaces of the neoliberal city and its promises of self-fashioning, Tshepo decks himself out in designer brands as part of his bid to grasp the elusive solidity that Tlali's hire-purchase customers had sought in the apartheid city. But the 'city of dreams' slips also through his fingers, and he delves increasingly into esoteric mythologies as if to produce a counter-reality to that of a metropolis that fails to nurture him.[9]

Duiker's title – 'The Quiet Violence of Dreams' – is suggestive of what Lauren Berlant describes as the condition of 'cruel optimism' (Berlant 2011) which sustains late capitalism. The global casualisation of labour has seen the proletariat replaced by the precariat, and it is this new class that Berlant finds to be caught in the cleft of 'cruel optimism'. The predicament of disposable labour has, however, long been prefigured in the racialised regimes of South African cities, and the earlier literature offers the well-established trope of the cannibal city to a new generation of writers for whom the condition of 'cruel optimism' takes on a particular intensity as an ostensibly new state takes shape in a global economy that precludes the redistribution of goods, and the dream of a better life is shown to consume character after character.

Some writers evade its grasp through an ethic of cynicism. Foremost here is Lesego Rampolokeng, whose 'sewer-bound poetics' (Rampolokeng 1999) cut through the conceit of the so-called 'rainbow nation' to reveal a revolution betrayed. For Rampolokeng, the city continues to devour African aspirations and black bodies through the extractive complex of 'Kimberley Joburg Cullinan'.[10] As he puts it baldly in a 'rant': 'Dreams come here to die' (Rampolokeng 2004). If there is an apparent progression from Serote's 'City Johannesburg' to Rampolokeng's 'Johannesburg my city', the prospect of the possessive is undermined by the consistent duplicity of the 'judas gold' with which it is '[p]aved' (Rampolokeng 2004).

A resonant critique is vocalised in *Outspoken* (2004) by Kgafela oa Magogodi, who describes himself as a 'riot'er, scholar, theatre director and spoken word warrior'. Magogodi returns to the figure of the 'chu chew train' gorging on 'human flesh' that was addressed by earlier migrants en route to the mines, and which he castigates for feeding off 'the fat' of the 'promised land' (Magogodi 2004: 6). Rendering its inexorable momentum as it cuts across the post-apartheid state, he notes that the 'gravy train' also 'chews' the very hands 'that laid the bricks to build mandela bridge' (Magogodi 2004: 6, 7): even this iconic infrastructure reaching across a divided city in a concrete manifestation of the hopes for a post-apartheid society is indicted for extending exploitation.

Showing up this society through a character who plays the system, rather than commenting critically on it, is Niq Mhlongo's *Dog Eat Dog* (2004). Seeking to elevate himself out of the hopeless squalor of the township through tertiary education, Mhlongo's protagonist Dingz is a consummate hustler: he plays up his family's poverty in the financial aid office, cries racial discrimination or evokes African traditions in a self-consciously white-dominated institution, and swindles a township-dweller by impersonating the new government. The latter scam is to secure a death certificate in support of his claim to having missed an exam in order to attend a family funeral. As Nuttall (2008: 214) notes: '[d]eath itself ... is his means of survival in the world to which he seeks to belong, the exchange currency, the city commodity, in which he deals'. In this updated version of the predicament informing *Sizwe Bansi Is Dead*, the death certificate comes to take the place of the 'Book of Life' and the township is located in a structurally similar position to the Bantustans established by the apartheid state: far from being bridged post-apartheid, the worlds of the city and the townships, as well as those of the townships and the suburbs, are shown to remain incommensurable.

Kopana Matlwa's novel *Coconut* (2007) uses a diptych structure to articulate the breach between those moving into luxury suburban estates and a majority still stuck in the cramped quarters to which apartheid had consigned them.[11] Each part is narrated by an adolescent girl living on either side of the chasm. Repelled by the 'stink of labourers' sweat' that lingers in train carriages, Fikile, who shares a one-room backyard shack with her lecherous uncle, harbours fantasies of driving past her fellow commuters 'in a sleek air-conditioned car' with the windows rolled up (Matlwa 2007: 134, 140). Ofilwe, in contrast, is ferried around the city in her family's luxury sedan, but, seeking human connection, gazes longingly through the glass at the informal traders who hawk their wares at intersections. She suffers what Zimbabwean author Tsitsi Dangarembga (1988) diagnosed as the 'nervous condition' produced in the 'native' by an oppressively sterile white world. Ofilwe's recovery, or 'detox' (Matlwa 2007: 48), lies in reconnecting with both the township and the countryside.

Sterility of another kind lodges in the suburban dwelling of a young couple from the hinterland of Cape Town who gained access to the early apartheid city by passing for white in Wicomb's novel *Playing in the Light*. The price exacted from them was a high one: the severance of connection to family and to sustaining country ways as they arrive on a 'one-way train ticket from platteland to town' (Wicomb 2006: 18). In a different dispensation, their daughter goes in search of her wrenched roots. Though the novel is not redemptive in tone, there is a luminous encounter with a rural raconteur dragging a 'ramshackle cart' who nearly collides with the protagonists on a country road before leaving them with a lantern made of coloured glass to take back to the city (Wicomb 2006: 88), and which might be seen to refract the titular 'playing in the light' from its earlier encoding as 'playing white'.[12]

In contrast to these enlivening recollections of connections that had been severed in the 'racial city', Fikile's aspiration to enter the airbrushed reality purveyed by glossy magazines remains unresolved by the plot of *Coconut*. Revealing the image of the 'city of dreams' that is reflected in them to be an injuriously seductive mirage, this lack of resolution is suggestive also of the confinement that many continue to experience in colonial-apartheid structures. *Room 207* (2007) by Kgebetli Moele expresses this condition as one of being trapped in the incessant script of a 'sad black story' (Moele 2007: 50).

The eponymous room of Moele's novel is in what used to be a hotel on the corner of Van der Merwe and Claim streets – an address which marks the intersecting interests of mining capital and Afrikaner nationalism. Says the narrator: 'it's been a temporary setting, since and until … I can't tell. What I do know is that we have spent eleven years staying there … This room is our safe haven during the lighted dark night of dream city' (Moele 2007: 13). The inner city having been abandoned by capital during the 1990s, Hillbrow becomes the new setting of the precarity previously imposed on the apartheid township. The would-be students and urbanites who share the room thus live in anticipation of the 'out-of-Hillbrow' (Moele 2007: 14) party that they plan to throw when they take up domicile in the suburbs or return triumphantly to their villages bearing some of the city's 'gold'. Having been drawn there by aspirations of upward mobility and fantasies of wealth, they are preoccupied during their stay in Hillbrow with hustling or what they simply call 'Johannesburging' (Moele 2007: 156), in a telling conflation of the 'dream city' and the 'money economy' (see Samson 2017: 30). By and large, however, they drop out of university or are financially precluded from pursuing their dreams. The narrator is finally forced to admit failure and returns home defeated. 'The vow that I took with myself, of driving myself out of Johannesburg, has been broken', he concludes bitterly; 'I'm still going out like I came in: taking a taxi out' (Moele 2007: 233).

Some writers draw on speculative genres to present 'critical dystopias' (Moylan 2000) of a city that offers such limiting scripts, or to cast visions of alternative urbanities. Duiker's posthumous novel, *The Hidden Star* (2006), for instance, takes a fabulous form to expose a subterranean world that partly references the gold mines on which the urban edifice is constructed but which is also imbued with redeeming rural ontologies (see Samuelson 2007: 254). In a reiteration of the earlier migrant poetics on the extractive city, a cannibalistic ogre preys on township children and puts them to work underground. Country ways are shown to offer alternative social practices to those forged on the foundational rapacity of the city and enable the children to reclaim the township as 'home':

> They've missed the township with its dusty streets … They've missed the squeezed-in shacks that leave little space for anything else, and the train that makes the tracks hum as it passes by.
> They've missed the township, because it is home.
>
> (Duiker 2006: 233)

As in *Coconut*, reconnection with the countryside provides a remedy for urban maladies rather than marking a failure to make it in the city, as it does in *Room 207*.

For the near-future city-dwellers of Lauren Beukes's dystopic *Moxyland* (2008), in contrast, the countryside offers little more than virtual wallpaper, selected at the click of a button. Beukes's cyberpunk portrayal of Cape Town shows the city disconnecting from the hinterland as it plugs into global networks, giving narrative content to Manuel Castells's (2010 [1997]: 166–169) observation that the network society of the information age connects places unevenly, producing a 'new geography of social exclusion' in which 'black holes' of misery expand between its radiant fibre-optic cables. This new global structure reprises the 'light city, dark city' model that produced apartheid's townships, as well as the relation that that regime established between white cities and black Bantustans. Castells (2004: 84, 89) indicates as much when he describes the structure in which 'depressed rural areas and urban shanty towns' are simply 'switched off' as one of 'technological apartheid'. In *Moxyland*, those who suffer 'disconnect' include the inhabitants of 'Rural' and 'loxion sprawl' (a reference to the apartheid-era 'locations' or townships). These are the 'abandoned subjects, relegated to the role of a "superfluous humanity"' of whom Mbembe (2017 [2013]: 1, 3) writes in his critique of what he describes as 'the becoming black of the world': '[i]f yesterday's drama of the subject was exploitation by capital, the tragedy of the multitude today is that they are unable to be exploited at all'.

Albeit projected into a post-race state, the residents of Beukes's city – as well as those who have been dumped in its constitutive outsides – might also be said to be trapped in an iterative 'sad, black story' as SIM-cards refigure the passbook to produce a society in which movement is meticulously monitored and marshalled.[13] The climax of the novel recapitulates a late-apartheid incident in which purple dye was sprayed on protestors in Cape Town to better identify and incarcerate them, while at the same time referencing the 'necropolitics' of the post-apartheid state: a virus is released to manage social unrest and the population is advised to present itself at designated vaccination centres; the character Tendeka refuses to submit to this operation of corporate-state power and meets a gruesome end while attempting to broadcast his annihilation in a protest whose efficacy remains ambiguous.[14] That Tendeka – the character who most espouses the ideal of the city as a place of assembly and who is most responsible to its outcast populations – also happens to be black re-inscribes race into the novel's response to the 'corporate apartheid' of 'neoliberalism' (Bethlehem 2014: 530). It is telling, also, that he is the character who does not survive this state.

The deadly persistence of race is indicated also in Sifiso Mzobe's *Young Blood* (2010), set in the city of Durban and Umlazi township. Sipho, the protagonist, is impelled to join a car hijacking racket by the foreclosed opportunities of the township. Echoing Abrahams's earlier indictment of the 'Manichean' city ('these streets and trees, almost, the clean air I breathed here, were: RESERVED FOR EUROPEANS ONLY' [Abrahams 1954: 164]), Sipho finds during his illicit incursions that '[t]he air you breathe changes in the suburbs. There are more trees than houses, more space than you can imagine' (Mzobe 2010: 46). Stolen vehicles enable him to move freely between township, suburb and city, and even awaken something in the city that seems to answer to his presence: 'The sound from the tailpipe reverberates off the buildings as if the high-rises, banks and chain stories have their own engines' (Mzobe 2010: 51). It is as if – to return to the imagery of Vilakazi's *Ezinkomponi* and Abrahams's *Mine Boy* – he becomes part of the great humming machine of the city, while refusing his assignation to the role of cog or flunky that can be exploited and discarded at will. Rather than being used by the city, the hijacker wrests control over its instruments. In a striking gesture, Sipho spins a car, literally writing himself onto the surface of the city: 'a few handbrake turns will turn the streets to pages, with tyres as black-inked pens' (Mzobe 2010). But this audacious act that might be seen to claim the city as 'oeuvre' in Lefebvre's sense is actually an extravagant mourning ritual to mark the death of a fellow car thief: the claim on the city that it would articulate is again a parlous one.

Ultimately, Sipho turns from the dangers of a life in crime to train as a motor mechanic who will repair and recycle vehicles. While presenting practices of appropriation and repurposing as central to crafting an urban subjectivity, the novel thus redirects them from illicit to legitimate practices. Other novels of this period invest less optimism in sanctioned urban activity, and return to peripatetic forms, pathological subjects and hustling as a way of writing themselves into the city. Restless and edgy, rather than tightly plotted, they evoke a sense of expectation without destination. No longer the literature of a nation-in-transition, these works speak instead to the long shadow cast by apartheid as well as to the dismal context of South Africa's belated emancipation. The latter included the derailing of the global 'narrative of liberation' after 1989 (West-Pavlov 2018a: 13) and the taking root locally of the HIV/AIDS pandemic, which now afflicts more people in South Africa than in any other country (as Frédéric le Marcis [2008: 170] puts it, '[p]eople obtained their freedom and fell sick at the same time').

What Themba described as the 'crepuscular' world of Sophiatown in the 1950s is in Songeziwe Mahlangu's *Penumbra* (2013) revised into the partial eclipse of the post-apartheid city by its exclusionary and segregated predecessor. Profiled as black, and thus an undesirable tenant, the narrator struggles to find accommodation in Cape Town, likening his condition to the workers who bus in and out of the suburbs each day; suffering a mental breakdown, he too eventually leaves the city by taxi, 'pass[ing] shanty-towns on the sides of the N2' on his way out. Realism blends into surrealism in this novel as the narrator's psychosis injects the city with ghastly visions that allow the reader to experience the cryptic hostility that it presents to him. The city that is received through the eyes of the glue-sniffing narrator of Masande Ntshanga's *The Reactive* (2014) similarly buckles into bewildering forms, even as both narratives are situated in mimetically mapped locales. In each, incessant movement combined with narrative stasis conveys the sense of characters being consumed by the streets that they would traverse. Ntshanga puns on exhaustion and vehicle emissions in a portrait of a metropolis that is largely composed of views from the minibus taxis that shuttle the urban poor across the vast distances that still separate many urban South Africans, and which devour the wages of the underpaid. The Cape Town that it renders is rimmed with a 'pink band' of smog, circumvented by container ships and strung together by the HIV support groups that the characters frequent. They do so not in search of solidarity, but rather as part of a scam. Most of the story is set before the belated public provision of anti-retroviral drugs in 2003, and their scam entails selling the life-prolonging pills that the narrator has secured through a private medical aim scheme contracted on compensation pay. Readers discover late in the narrative that he became a 'reactive' (i.e. tested positive for HIV) after infecting himself in the labs where he worked as an act of expiation for what he experiences as his culpability in his younger brother's death during his ritual initiation into manhood in 1993 – a date that lends this failed rite of passage allegorical resonance. A decade into the new democracy, the narrator is reminded by his uncle that he has come of age and is summoned back to his kin. After completing his own communal rite of passage in the countryside, he returns to a revised relationship with the city. No longer recklessly orienting himself towards 'Last Life', nor maintaining the hopeless hope of immunity, he is now prepared to live up to his name, Lindanathi, which means 'wait with us'.

A similar arc gives shape to Perfect Hlongwane's episodic novella of ideas, *Jozi* (2013). Madness, death and disease stalk the streets of Hlongwane's inner city, in which the precarity of black urban life produces similar novel challenges to those addressed in Mpe's second person narrative voice: the narrator shifts abruptly from the first to the third person as various characters are felled by violent crime and illness. *Jozi* opens by reiterating the trope of the inner city as a 'heartless place ... a monster that swallows people whole ... chews them up and spits them out'; it is the 'city of dreams' only to the extent that it is 'a place where dreams come to die' (Hlongwane 2013: np). The penultimate episode even offers a version in precis of the plot of *Cry, the Beloved Country*. But instead of joining Paton in advocating flight from the city, *Jozi* grapples with characters' culpability in the reproduction of the callousness that haunts its streets and moves towards finding other affective orientations to the city than those offered by the alluring yet consuming 'city of dreams'. As with *The Reactive* and some of the other post-apartheid texts that reflect on the failed promises of democracy, *Jozi* ends not with Themba's (1972b) 'will to die' – though death certainly beckons – but rather with a commitment to community and a call to care that this study returns to in conclusion.

The citadel and the polis

Traffic in Joburg is like the democratic process. Every time you think it's going to get moving and take you somewhere, you hit another jam. There used to be shortcuts you could take through the suburbs, but they've closed them off, illegally: gated communities fortified like privatised citadels.

– Lauren Beukes, *Zoo City* (2010)

The unfettered movement embodied in the figure of Jonker's child traversing the world without a pass is repeatedly shown to be arrested again by an 'architecture of fear' that is redesigning the polis of assembly into a conglomeration of citadels (Bremner 2010: 180).[15] Sealed up under the sign of private property, these exclusionary enclaves turn away from and impede public space in order to shore up the interests of the moneyed.[16] The liberated city is again cast as a warzone: hippos may have left the townships, but the suburbs have been militarised with private security personnel and fortified structures. Vladislavić (2006a: 54) speculates that '[a] stranger, arriving one evening in the part of Joburg [he] call[s] home, would think that it had been struck by some calamity, that every last person had fled. There is no sign of life. Behind the walls, the houses are ticking like bombs'.

While the armoured character of South African cities may be distinctive, they are also more broadly indicative of how the uneven distribution of social goods under neoliberal conditions have produced 'cities of walls' and 'carceral archipelagos' across the globe, and particularly in the postcolonial south (Caldeira 2000; Soja 1997: 22). As Theresa Caldeira (2000: 1–2) shows, these 'new forms of spatial segregation and social discrimination' thwart the processes of 'democratic consolidation' that cities such as São Paolo or Johannesburg might be expected to support. This interest in the city as the foreclosed locus of the political is itself a significant claim. Ananya Roy (2009: 821) has lamented that global urban theory tends to focus on cities as spaces of 'economic competitiveness' rather than viewing them as a 'terrain of political struggle and subject-making' or as theatres of democracy. In its emphasis on reactivating the city as polis, South African literature – like other literatures of the global south – offers an important corrective.[17] At the same time, manifesting the fortress city in hyperbolic form, urban South Africa also provides 'privileged insight into the workings of the world at large' (Comaroff & Comaroff 2012: 1) in a time of deepening social inequality or what is sometimes simply called 'global apartheid'.

Grappling with this global condition in exaggerated form, South African literatures trouble the ways in which these new urban structures seek to detach from the implications of the democratic state while observing also the deprivation suffered by those who sequester themselves behind walls, trading sociality for security. The protection offered by the citadel is, moreover, shown to be superficial or even imperilling to its inhabitants as much as to society at large. For instance, in Gordimer's *The House Gun* (1998) it is the ready availability of a domestic weapon that brings ruin to a commune which had promised to realise the desegregating and un-closeting possibilities of the post-apartheid dispensation. Security features offer no defence against a harm that comes from within or is reproduced in the fortified divisions between privilege and penury.

Gordimer explicitly situates her modernist novel outside the burgeoning crime-and-detection genre, but many of the growing number of these popular works convey a similar message as they craft identifiably South African forms within global conventions.[18] The emerging international configuration of the 'exopolis' – Edward Soja's (1997: 22) term for the city turned 'inside-out and outside-in' – is also given local content in cities like Johannesburg where the flight of capital towards its edges is part of a reaction to the 'loss of the racial city' (Mbembe 2008: 63). Vladislavić explores this form in *The Exploded View* (2004) in which the new citadel complexes that enable their residents to evade the democratic state include incongruous developments such 'Villa Toscana, a little prefabricated Italy in the veld', replete with the ersatz ramparts designed to give it 'the medieval treatment' (Vladislavić 2004: 3, 7). The style displays what Mbembe (2008: 62) describes as an 'architecture of hysteria', which is 'characterised by the attachment to a lost object that used to provide comfort' – hence Matlwa's diagnosis of a Tuscan-style gated community as the diseased bastion of white hegemony in the novel *Coconut*.[19]

Vladislavić anticipated the psychic structure of this neurotic city in *The Restless Supermarket* when his protagonist attempts to withdraw from the diversifying streets of Hillbrow into 'Café Europa'. In *The Exploded View*, he again experiments with novel possibilities to craft an appropriate vehicle for the exopolis as it takes shape in the 'frontier zone' that is the post-apartheid city (see Bremner 2010: 170). Comprised of four fragments that are connected only in the most precarious way by characters who are shown '[d]riving, always driving' (Vladislavić 2004: 6), the narrative takes its form from the city that it portrays: fractured and dispersed, moving edgily outwards and held together only by highways (see Helgesson 2006: 28). This depiction of a disjointed city that is reassembled only through traffic is suggestive of the ways in which what the sociologists Mimi Sheller and John Urry (2004: 204) call 'automobility', with its 'distinct combination of flexibility and coercion', has 'reshaped citizenship and the public sphere'. Rather than centred upon the town square or activated in the pages of newspapers and novels, the community depicted in *The Exploded View* is imagined through the 'laws of traffic' that issue in radio bulletins reporting on collisions and pile-ups and which are received in each quasi-private vehicular capsule (Vladislavić 2004: 160, 161).[20] The performance of good citizenship is reduced therein to maintaining the regulated flow, with no space afforded for deliberation or dissension.

Presenting a city comprised of highways, hotel rooms, supermarkets and the vacuous units of misplaced architectural styles, Vladislavić shows Johannesburg to be increasingly absorbed into what anthropologist Marc Augé (1995) defines as 'non-place'. In contrast to the 'organically social' practices that might materialise on neighbourhood streets, these transitory spaces that characterise 'supermodernity' are determined by 'their "instructions for use", which may be prescriptive ..., prohibitive ... or informative' (Augé 1995: 94, 96). As such 'non-places' come to 'colonize ever larger chunks of public space' (Bauman 2000: 102), the post-apartheid city continues to speak in a monologue like its colonial-apartheid predecessor. It is now, however, by turns both injunctive and seductive in its address as the signs that regulated traffic according to an assigned racial group are replaced by anodyne interpellations of the individualised yet 'formulaic' consumer (Vladislavić 2004: 31). One of Vladislavić's characters is in the enterprise of erecting billboards that present enticing simulacra of building projects that are themselves simulacra; it is, as he boasts, 'big business' (Vladislavić 2004: 173). That he is hijacked and, presumably, killed beneath one advertising a luxury lodge is indicative of the relationship between consumption, crime and these new urban constructions.[21] Certainly, his presence there in search of a missing cellular phone is telling of a thwarted desire for connection and communication in a city that is both compartmentalised and 'edgy' (Kruger 2013).[22]

Beukes's *Moxyland*, in which cellular phones are the new medium of social control, magnifies the citadel through future projection. The fragmentation that the 'citadelisation' of the city induces is again rendered formally: the story is narrated by four distinct characters whose relationships are largely transactional. The city that they inhabit is composed of total-lifestyle establishments housing residents who need 'never ventur[e] out on the street' (Beukes 2008: 67), and is itself an enclave cut off from its surroundings. Clues on how to read this city are offered on entry when one of the four characters catches an underground train that is suspended on 'a skin of seawater ... in the watery bowels of Cape Town' (Beukes 2008: 1). Floating in 'the space of flows' (Castells 2004), as it were, this urban enclave that references the enclosures of colonialism and apartheid is also a product of the global state of 'software capitalism' that Bauman (2000) calls 'liquid modernity'.

If these new urban forms seem extraneous to the grounded realities of South African cities, it is salient to note that the model 'fortress city' to which Bauman refers in elaborating 'liquid modernity' is the Heritage Park development on the outskirts of Cape Town: a self-enclosed town said to be inspired by the medieval walled city, but which finds its prototype in South Africa's more recent history. At the time of Bauman's writing, it was still a planned development, but it has since been realised according to its exclusionary designs; making local and global headlines in 2006, it evidently informed Beukes's fictional projection. Transporting readers into this world on the 'corporate line [that] shushes through the tunnels' beneath the city, 'send[ing] plumes of seawater arcing' as it pulls into 'the Waterfront Exec station' (Beukes 2008: 1), *Moxyland* is suggestive of how the fragmented surface of the city is buoyed up by an underflow of capital.

A related way of thinking about 'Moxyland' that is encouraged by this opening image is through the practice of 'offshoring' (Urry 2014). Offshoring, argues John Urry, is the practice by which the 'money economy' in its neoliberal phase performs the 'willed concealment' (Simmel in Urry 2014) that a prior state had enacted through the infrastructure of the mine shaft and labour compound.[23] Nuttall and Mbembe, who identified the definitional 'dialectic between the underground, the surface and the edges' (Mbembe and Nuttall 2008: 17) of the African metropolis, take up Urry's concept to propose the figure of the 'offshore city' for understanding the modes of 'urban encapsulation' by which 'profit is disentangled from the place in which extraction happens' (Nuttall & Mbembe 2015: 320, 321). Characterised by 'the dissolution of public space', such urban formations can be seen to undermine democracy itself (Castells 2004: 91; Urry 2014).

In *Moxyland*, the closely monitored movements of characters across an access-controlled city contrast with the deregulated flows of capital and commodities in and out of it. This tension animates many a novel. Trafficking plots preoccupy a high proportion of the crime thrillers produced during this period,[24] and also inform literary fiction, with various works pointing again to the '*pas de duex*' of licit and illicit economies in the neoliberal postcolony (Comaroff & Comaroff 2006: 6). Zinaid Meeran's *Saracen at the Gates* (2010), for instance, shows how the operations of human trafficking run parallel to and even support those of speculative capitalism, and vice versa. Both are extractive and offshoring practices, and *Saracen at the Gates* shows them to manifest locally in enclave urbanism. Meeran's protagonist, who sports with an Indian Ocean Rim Subtropical Natural Extraction financial portfolio given to her by her father ('I plundered the subtropics ... [sending] hundreds of thousands of rand flying from one fragile economy to another with a flick of the mouse'), is said to suffer 'pedestrian aphasia' (Meeran 2010: 299, 256) as she races between the exclusive nodes that compose her city. But she comes to recognise that these enclaves are enabled by and in turn maintain a transnational network of exploitation in which she is implicated.

Joining a group of graffiti taggers who style themselves 'Saracens', Meeran's protagonist notes how billboards 'leer' at passing motorists as they crash 'in waves against concrete overpasses' (Meeran 2010: 152). These waves – like *Moxyland*'s underground trains – again reference the condition of 'liquid modernity'. This condition, Bauman (2000: 39) argues, is characterised not by the invasion of the 'private' by the 'public' – as was the modus operandi of the colonial-apartheid state that legislated where residents could live and with whom they might enjoy intimate relations – but rather by the saturation of 'public space' with private interests. The depoliticising nature of 'liquid modernity' is again evident in *Moxyland*: repressive measures may be deployed to keep its residents in line, but the giant adboards that stud the city, peddling private fantasies of consumption, co-opt most of them so effectively that brute force is seldom required and the prospect of mass resistance appears at best uncertain. It is such situations that lead Bauman (2000: 39) to conclude that the task facing critique today is no longer that of 'the defense of private autonomy', but rather the need 'to refurnish and repopulate the public space'.

Graffiti provides a figure through which *Moxyland* and *Saracen at the Gates* stage this refurnishing and repopulating as they present characters short-circuiting adboards or tagging on flyovers as ways of re-activating publicness in the city.[25] Addressing passing strangers and provoking debate (including about conceptions of private property), rather than seeking to elicit the private desires that consumption feeds, this writing on the city produces what Nancy Fraser (1990: 57) describes as zones of 'discursive interaction' without at the same time reproducing the exclusions encoded in the terms 'rational' or 'virtuous' through which Habermas (1989) defines the public sphere. In other words, it can be said to convene counter-publics while jamming the circuits through which official culture – or that which purports to represent *the* public and which is increasingly the role assumed by consumer culture – projects itself. Specifically, graffiti provides a compelling trope for how texts participate in the work of inscribing the city as 'oeuvre' (Lefebvre 1996: 117), thus claiming participatory power to shape what the city means and how it functions, rather than being satisfied with the diminished right to consume (in) the city.

Such writing is part of 'the struggle of the polis to create the city as a meaningful place' (Castells 2004: 92) – a place that is both 'playful' and 'conflictual' (Harvey 2012: x) – rather than a sequence of non-places through which capital transits or a series of citadels in which it accumulates. Another means by which the literature opens the monologue of the official city (whether injunctive or seductive) into a 'dialogue' (Vladislavić 2006a: 53) is through what De Certeau (1984: 99, 97, 98) refers to as 'walking in the city': the 'pedestrian enunciation' as a 'spatial acting-out of the place' that 'transforms each spatial signifier into something else' and which creates different possibilities – or itineraries – to those imposed by town planners; it is a way of writing with one's footsteps another city to that which has been traced out on the official blueprint. Such enunciations infuse the literature of this period, in which perambulating narrators convey readers along the groves of particular urban pathways, naming each street or landmark that they pass while infusing them with unofficial histories. '[A]rticulat[ing] a sentence that [their] steps compose' (De Certeau 1984: 104), this prose becomes again a collaboration between the writer and the city, as it was for Themba before Sophiatown was razed.

Mhlongo's *Dog Eat Dog* notably intertwines the tropes of graffiti and walking. As Dingz moves across Johannesburg, Mhlongo reproduces the writing that he finds scrawled on toilet doors, emblazoned on taxis, born on banners by protestors and held up at traffic lights by beggars. The reader is thus positioned alongside Dingz to receive and respond to the city-as-oeuvre. The array of contrasting and even conflicting messages they encounter recompose both the city and the page that represents a surface on which intersecting and diverging counter-publics contend with one another in an exchange that runs athwart the signs erected by the official culture. Publics, notes Michael Warner (2002: 50), come into being 'in relation to texts and their circulation'. As various urban texts are drawn into this novel that was itself remarkable for being a local bestseller in a country with a small readership, it too becomes a public with which the reader is invited to interact.

The 138 nonfictional pieces comprising Vladislavić's *Portrait with Keys: Joburg & what-what* (2006a) are similarly gathered into what we might think of as a textual polis. Vladislavić's title puns on a portrayal that opens the city to readers by disclosing how certain residents – confronted with the shifting demographics that disturbed the protagonist of *The Restless Supermarket* – huddle behind bolted gates as if they are the wardens of their own gaol.[26] The narrator's walks often terminate abruptly before such defensive structures; the city, he observes, is 'vanish[ing] behind walls' (Vladislavić 2006a: 49). The fragmented form of this portrait conveys something of the compartmentalisation of a city in which it is 'impossible for certain ... paths to cross' (Vladislavić 2006a: 12). But it also permits the reorganisation of textual and urban space, as readers are invited to plot alternative itineraries across its pages and thus to reactivate the 'conversation' between 'the way and the walker' (Vladislavić 2006a: 53) that the citadel interrupts. Drawing inspiration from De Certeau, Vladislavić (2006a: 166) plots various digressions which step out a different city to that taking shape around automobility – one in which '[e]very new building ... has secure, controlled, vehicle-friendly entrances and exit. The well-heeled – who naturally are also the well-wheeled – should be able to reach point B without setting foot in the street'. Refusing these designs, Vladislavić explicitly performs what De Certeau calls '"long poem of walking"' (qtd. Vladislavić 2006a: 53) that 'manipulates spatial organizations no matter how panoptic they may be' (De Certeau 1984: 101). (We see something similar at work in novels such as *Welcome to Our Hillbrow* and *Jozi* in which the proper names of mining capital and the 'racial city' that have been used to map urban space are 'empt[ied]-out' by perambulating narrators, such that the streets they designate 'become liberated spaces that can be occupied' [De Certeau 1984: 104–105]).

Vladislavić's portrait of Johannesburg is comprised of notes gleaned during his own walks across the city and from his perusal of its texts. In the essay 'X marks the spot' (2006b), he recalls how he began writing under the encouragement of a schoolteacher, who advised keeping the 'writer's notebook' from which it would later be assembled (Vladislavić 2006b: 125). Using a turn of phrase that is redolent of the 'money economy', Vladislavić (2006b: 125, 126) claims that these notebooks eluded 'the tyrannical currency of the syllabus' and require him also to 'step out of the crush in the mall'. His prose, he says, germinates not in the individual notes per se, which 'contain every conceivable kind of material'; instead, composition occurs in 'the congruence or clash' between two or more entries (Vladislavić 2006b: 126). In the process, the distinct voices and registers comprising the notebooks are 'brought on the same level: the surface of the page. Like immigrants given a new suit of clothes and a passport, they assume democratic citizenship of the same textual world. They are able to approach one another, to argue and interact' (Vladislavić 2006b: 126). This textual polis might be seen to articulate that which his narratives seek to enact or evoke in urban space, or it may offer refuge to modes of publicness that have been evicted from the city proper.

It is significant that Vladislavić likens the texts interacting in his writing to immigrants, rather than nationals, assuming democratic citizenship. Like other writing from this period, this is a claim that seeks to realise the polis while at the same time responding to xenophobic attempts to expel other Africans from the post-apartheid state, and particularly from its cities (the echoes of the apartheid regime's attempt to cast black South Africans as foreigners in order to exclude them from the city and ultimately the country are painfully obvious, as is the failure to recognise the labour of the many transnational migrants who also toiled in its mines).

Beukes takes up these concerns in her second novel, *Zoo City* (2010), from which the epigraph to this section is drawn. Ruing how paths across the suburbs have been 'closed ... off, illegally' to produce 'gated communities', this noir fantasy is centred on Hillbrow, which is now imagined as a 'ghetto warren' (Beukes 2010: 85, 205) populated by people who have been 'animalled' (the narrator has been gifted or cursed with a sloth). Two strands spool out from this centre and converge in the figure of the crocodile: there is the rags-to-riches story of a singing twin sensation from the Valley of the Thousand Hills that ends in the jaws of an albino crocodile familiar lurking beneath their manager's mansion; and there is the story of refugees seeking to cross a riverine national border that is said to be patrolled by these reptilian 'sentries' (Beukes 2010: 307). Together they present Johannesburg as a cannibalistic white city that closes its doors against the rest of the continent (the metaphor depends somewhat on the sobriquet of PW Botha, who earned the title '*Die Groot Krokodil*' [lit. 'the big crocodile'] from his supporters for the intransigent manner in which he presided over the late apartheid state).

Buekes's eponymous ghetto is inhabited by people marked with visible signs of misconduct and who are disproportionately foreign. Their misdemeanours are then measured against those of a city that has consumed labour from across the region while excluding its subjects from sharing in its goods. These goods have instead been secreted into 'privatised citadels' scattered across the suburbs while the inner city mutates into a high-rise squat governed by security companies who have been enlisted in service to corporate profit rather than public accountability. The tactic of this novel, in the face of the urban condition that it represents, is again to reassemble the polis within itself, which it does by bringing distinct orders of textuality into contact on its pages. The narrative is interspersed with 419 scam emails, police records, media reports, chatroom discussion boards, online film reviews and excerpts from a fictional series of interviews with imprisoned 'zoos', some of which were written by other authors. Presented in different fonts, as are those in *Dog Eat Dog*, these texts are neither assimilated into the novel nor mediated by it but are instead left to collide in a cacophony of counterclaims.

Beukes's protagonist is, like Mhlongo's Dingz, a hustler. Her scam exploits the gullibility of strangers and the tragedies that have driven asylum seekers to her city. When, at the end of the novel, she renounces it in favour of embracing the stranger, she marks a turn that becomes an increasingly vital theme in the literature. While hustling – and hijacking – are taken up in these works as modes of appropriation through which characters lay claim to the city, they are both ultimately shown to reproduce the city-of-death and to feed the 'dog eat dog' morality of its 'money economy'.[27] Indeed, as Mda's *Black Diamonds* (2009) and Mhlongo's *Way Back Home* (2013) suggest, the true hustlers of the post-apartheid city are the so-called 'tenderpreneurs' (a portmanteau from 'tender' and 'entrepreneur') who use political connections to secure government contracts in order to sequester themselves in the enclaves of the old and new elite.

Hospitable cities and the city as hospice

Here we live. Here, where without
Compassion, comradeship, tenderness
It is hell.

– Jeremy Cronin, 'This City' (1997)

Rather than seeking to lay their own claim on it, some writers have begun to turn away from the consuming and enclaving city of speculative finance and of licit or illicit hustling. They are drawn instead to the enlivening relations that cities can also host. Theorising the metropolis at the dawn of the twentieth century, Simmel (2004 [1903]: 15) found that the sensory stimulation to which its frenetic activity exposed city-dwellers induced a 'blasé attitude'. Literature emerging from the early twenty-first century 'Afropolis' (Nuttall & Mbembe 2008) indicates a notable movement in which such nonchalance is replaced by an attitude of answerability to fellow urbanites, to the city itself and to the world beyond. This writing begins to reimagine the city in profound ways: not as a place of prospects, but rather as one of community, conviviality and care.[28] Relinquishing the alluring figure of 'dream city', it searches for ways of living on amidst the death of dreams – and, when even this proves too much to hope for, it attends to the work of dying well, and of embracing the uncurable and the dead.

Jeremy Cronin's reflection on Johannesburg begins to point the way to this city of caritas and association. In a state that is being hijacked by tenderpreneurs, it calls instead for 'tenderness' (Cronin 1999 [1997]: 118).[29] Enjoined to 'comradeship' are those who shuttle – '[w]indows uptight, door-knobs down' – through the streets of a 'heart torn out, suburbed, scattered, shopping-malled' city still circled by 'the dark moons' of the townships. 'Compassion' is submitted as that which could release this 'screwed up, wounded city, bruised / By the abusings of its past' from the iteration of 'hell' (Cronin 1999 [1997]: 118).

While commenting on the private security detail that reinstates the apartheid city in the form of the citadel, Cronin refers also to the time he spent in Lusaka as a member of the exiled ANC/SACP alliance. This passing reference resonates with what will become a growing complaint against post-apartheid South Africa from across and within its borders. It concerns the xenophobic treatment with which non-national Africans have been met in this state, and particularly in its cities in which there have been sporadic instances and occasional country-wide campaigns of violence directed against them (the reasons vary, but most typically include non-nationals being blamed for urban crime, the spread of HIV and taking local jobs or houses, amongst other projected ills). Following a series of such assaults, the Mozambican writer Mia Couto (2015) addressed an open letter to then President Jacob Zuma, reminding him of the refuge that he had found in Maputo during the struggle and of the high price that was exacted by the apartheid regime for the support that Mozambique had offered to the liberation movement (a burden shared by other 'frontline states', including Zambia in which Cronin had sheltered); he recalls also the migrants who toiled in South Africa's mines, concluding: '[t]here is no wealth in your country that does not carry the contribution of those who are today coming under attack'.

After the first eruptions of violence against Africans perceived as 'foreigners' in the new nation, including an incident in which a Mozambican and two Senegalese died after being thrown from a train in Johannesburg,[30] two narratives published in 2000 – a novel and a collaborative work of nonfiction – begin to enquire into the forms of accommodation extended to those who have crossed South Africa's land border. The first, the novel *Skyline* by Patricia Schonstein Pinnock, takes its name from an apartment block in inner-city Cape Town that hosts a cast of characters from across the continent along with others abjected from national life – including an interracial blind couple, a transgendered couple, refugees from Nazi Germany and the girl narrator and her sister, who are abandoned by their father and neglected by an alcoholic mother. As the narrator explains: '[m]ost of the people who live here are illegal immigrants and refugees from the rest of Africa ... Not many of them have the right to be here and most of them carry forged papers or pay bribes to stay in the country. They arrive from all over Africa by taxi, by bus, by train. Some hitch rides on overland transporters. Many just walk' (Pinnock 2000: 8). Just as the young Nelson Mandela had been attracted by the opportunities that the city appeared to offer, these transnational migrants are now said to have been drawn to the promise issued by 'Mr Mandela's country' (Pinnock 2000: 9). The new polity, however, rejects them on similar terms to those by which the apartheid state's 'homeland' policy expelled Africans from its cities: '[t]hey must go back to their own country' (Pinnock 2000: 10) is the axiom that the girl picks up from the street.

Ekphrasis provides the structuring device by which she instead houses their stories in her narrative: concluding each chapter is a description of a painting that presents a vignette featuring one or other of the members of the transnational community of Skyline, the places from whence they have come and the arduous journeys they have undertaken in search of sanctuary. The artist, as readers discover late in the story, is Bernard, an asylum seeker from war-torn Mozambican who sold flags at a traffic intersection and who befriended, and even acted as father to, the narrator before being killed in a xenophobic attack.

Finding Mr Madini (2000) by Jonathan Morgan and the Great African Spider Writers also seeks to craft a narrative able to house the stories of those who are not accommodated in post-apartheid cities, including unprocessed or denied asylum seekers, those who have been designated 'illegal immigrants' and the homeless. To achieve this form of hospitality, the creative project is recast from a thriller authored by Morgan and populated by stereotypical characters – including a Nigerian crack dealer and Ghanaian street barber – to the curation of a collaborative and composite work of life writing. Assembled in it are narratives workshopped by a collective that names itself 'the Great African Spider Writers': their stories converge in Johannesburg while the 'legs' of each reach out across the country, continent and globe. Together, they are said to construct in writing a home with windows that open outwards, and which stand in contrast to the 'architecture of fear' that the thriller form – as the conventional purveyor of 'crime talk' – might be seen to design, as well as with the barracks to which labour migrants had been consigned in the colonial-apartheid city.

Other novels stage hospitality through their address. Moele's narrator, for instance, invites readers to '[o]pen the door' (Moele 2007: 13) and enter the eponymous Room 207 before taking them on a walking tour around his locale. Mpe's 'welcome' goes even further: it functions as an extended speech-act that opens up a shared city – '*our* Hillbrow' – rather than posing as the host inviting the stranger into the home. This shift, subtle though it may be, is a significant one. Offering hospitality can be a generous gesture, but, as Jacques Derrida (2010) shows, it can also be a hostile statement of ownership and mastery. At stake in the offer of hospitality, then, is the relation of the post-apartheid state to the rest of the continent and, indeed, to its own past. The ubiquitous statement cited in *Skyline* – '[t]hey must go back to their own country' – reiterates the exclusions of the apartheid city while designating non-national Africans as 'foreign'.

In a recent response to such statements, Mbembe (a Cameroonian citizen who has long been resident in South Africa) puts it thus: 'I am not a foreigner in South Africa – or anywhere else on this continent' (2019). While the 'machinery' of the apartheid city 'has been partially dismantled', he observes that 'its habitus has remained alive' in the xenophobia of the new state: '[t]oday, many black "foreign nationals" are at the receiving end of this violence originally designed to discipline and domesticate black South Africans' (Mbembe 2019). Leaving aside the contest of claiming and counterclaiming, Mbembe (2019) emphasises instead the 'right of abode', which he locates in the responsibility toward '*caring and caretaking*' for the earth and all who inhabit it, 'humans and non-humans' alike, and in which such custodianship is undertaken 'in memory of those who came before and on behalf of those who were still to come'. Mbembe (2019) refers here to an ethos learnt from 'narratives of autochthony' that he had imbibed in rural Cameroon, but novelists such as Duiker, Pinnock, Beukes, Mpe and Hlongwane evoke it also in the densely populated, inner-city neighbour-hoods of Johannesburg and Cape Town.

Duiker's character Tshepo exits the 'quiet violence' of 'dream city' and moves to Hillbrow where he devotes himself to the care of street-children and finds belonging through living with 'foreigners, illegal and legal immi-grants, what black South Africans call makwere-kwere with derogatory and defiant arrogance': 'I feel at home with them', he says, 'because they are trying to find a home in our country' (Duiker 2001: 454). Making home *with* Africa, rather than inviting Africa *into* South African cities, is presented by this conclusion as a means of reassembling a fractured urban world and ministering to the wounds inflicted '[b]y the abusings of its past' (Cronin 1997 [1999]: 118). So too for the creative act depicted in *Skyline*: when the narrator arrogates to herself the role of representing refugees, she tends to reproduce victimhood, but she too is unhomed in this plot; by reconceiv-ing of 'hospitality as mutual homing', the novel deconstructs the binary of citizen versus foreigner, and that of the host versus the guest (Fasselt 2011: 181). This ethos of 'living-with' others that, for Simone (2018: 123), char-acterises 'Southern cities',[31] is extended also to non-humans in Beukes's *Zoo City* through the fantastical figure of the 'aposymbiont' (from the roots 'apo', or 'separate', and 'symbiont', meaning 'living together', it identi-fies the 'zoos' as distinct organisms bound in mutually beneficial relation): sustaining life in this fabulist Hillbrow is shown to depend on responsibility towards and care for non-citizen as well as non-human others. Cityness is thus reimagined as the locus of transnational, multispecies community.

These and other works can be seen to nudge hospitality toward a more egalitarian conviviality. Francis Nyamnjoh (2017: 262, 263), another Cameroonian intellectual based in South Africa, proclaims the value of conviviality, noting that it 'implies a sense of accommodating togetherness beyond mere *tolerance*' and is 'imbued with the spirit of togetherness, inter-penetration, interdependence and intersubjectivity'. It is, he observes, an attitude honed 'in the very cramped nature of inner cities, emerging in the precariousness of living together under tense circumstances' and in which people depend on 'mutual support to get by' (Nyamnjoh 2017: 264). This attitude is evoked in the stories that Mphahlele set in the slum-like condi-tions of early apartheid Newclare, which emphasise the interdependencies – and, indeed, the festivities – sustaining residents of the 'dilapidated houses [standing] cheek-by-jowl as if to support one another in the event of disas-ter' (Mphahlele 2001 [1956b]: 133). *Welcome to Our Hillbrow* reanimates such conviviality in the post-apartheid city. As Nyamnjoh (2006: 75) has argued, the novel imagines 'a more flexible citizenship informed less by rigid geographies of apartheid than by histories of relationships, intercon-nectedness, networks and conviviality'. Because 'migrants serve as bridges of conviviality between communities, civilisations and cultures' (Nyamnjoh 2006: 75), they provide the very infrastructure of the hospitable city, rather than being simply accommodated or tolerated in it. This infrastructure, as Mpe's narrative emphasises, also bridges the apartheid divide between the city and the countryside, as well as the ontological border between the liv-ing and the deceased (see Samuelson 2007). It serves ultimately, as Hoad (2006: 126) argues of the novel itself, to 'move its protagonists and read-ers from a xenophobic, exoticizing position in relation to the African HIV/ AIDS pandemic to the melancholia of a cosmopolitanism that can embrace other people's dead'.

Hlongwane's *Jozi* comes to rest resonantly on an embrace of other peo-ple's dying. It opens, as we have seen, with the by-now conventional cri-tique of the city as the place where 'dreams come to die'. The cannibal city is presented in various scenes of urban violence: one person is killed for a paltry amount of cash while a passer-by crosses the street, '[t]oo scared, or unwilling, to help' (Hlongwane 2013: np); a petty thief dies at the hands of a vigilante mob with which the narrator becomes unwittingly complicit; and, he is soon after murdered during a mugging. These scenes render the 'hardness' and 'indifference' that Simmel (2004 [1903]: 13, 16, 15) locates in the metropolis that is organised around the 'money economy', and which 'expresses all qualitative differences of things in terms of "How much?"' Yet even as it evokes the negative encoding of the city that saw earlier writ-ers such as RRR Dhlomo and Paton counselling flight from it, *Jozi* remains resolute in its urban attachments while at the same time being responsible to rural ones.

The urban sex-workers that Dhlomo's novella blamed for transferring disease to the countryside are here shown to remit their earnings to families across southern African and are thus recognised as enabling the survival of many a rural community:

> nearly all of what they make is sent home to KwaZulu, Eastern Cape, Limpopo, Swaziland, Zimbabwe, Mozambique, Zambia, and so on. That money is feeding and burying grandmothers, fathers, aunties ... you name it. It's raising and schooling brothers, sisters, cousins, nieces and nephews.
>
> (Hlongwane 2013: np)

Rather than 'an instance of "degenerate" city hustling', theirs 'is an example of networks of care' (Samson 2017: 50). The character who observes these networks had, he confessed, hoped that the women were instead saving their money 'to make a clean break'; their altruism, he recognises, means that 'many of them are never going to get out. Most likely, they'll just die of Aids' (Hlongwane 2013: np). This sobering analysis is delivered in the opening pages of the novella as a 'highly contentious point' (Hlongwane 2013: np). Seemingly functioning to invite the reader into a zone of deliberation – a public that is both convened and mirrored by the novella – it sets up a tension between sustaining care and death that the novella will return to and ultimately collapse in its concluding image of the city as hospice.

'Theorists of modernity', notes Le Marcis (2008: 170), 'regard the city as the place par excellence for the realization of the individual'; thus, urban suffering is understood by Simmel and others as the effect of 'isolation and anonymity'. But in cities such as Johannesburg, 'the body afflicted with AIDS itself constitutes an archetypal figure ... in its search for care and for sanctuary' (Le Marcis 2008: 171). Redrawing the map of the city as outlined by these 'suffering' bodies, Le Marcis (2008: 175) asks readers to consider how the city might be seen 'to show itself' in the hospice (rather than in 'the shape of the bar, the café, the restaurant, the shop, or the motorway') where 'it appears as a final attempt to render the last moments of life humane'. *Jozi* undertakes such a redrawing of the urban map, allowing the city 'to show itself' in the form of a hospice.

Its initial narrator having been felled on the street, the novella concludes by homing in Senzo, who was previously a secondary character. Once an infamous 'conman', he has grown fatigued with the now de rigueur 'disillusionment' that followed the 'high hopes' of the national 'miracle'. Himself suffering from terminal AIDS, Senzo's story ends with him caring for the dying by offering counselling to his fellows in the hospice. In so doing, he explicitly redirects the moral of *An African Tragedy*, Dhlomo's earlier cautionary tale of urban selfishness and vice: '[i]f the story of my life is to be a tragedy, he thought, then I will make it a useful tragedy' (Hlongwane 2013: np). Concludes the novel: '[w]hat would be would be, but he would do what he could to redeem the time in the days that were left to him. A deadly virus was in his body, but hope was in it also' (Hlongwane 2013: np). Through the figure of the city as hospice, Hlongwane thus returns to the city of death, but locates it in a very different setting and ethic to that of the consuming mine. At the same time, the fact that the setting is a hospice, not a hospital, and that the care which Senzo offers and receives is palliative rather than curative, radically redirects the meaning of the 'hope' that provides this final orientation toward the urban, drawing it emphatically away from the glittering pavements of the city of dreams. Refusing the kind of city that is built upon extraction and consumption, *Jozi* concludes instead with a melancholy yet tender gesture towards urban community and care.

This recasting of the city as a place of attachment and responsibility, rather than one of autonomy and freedom, is a significant intervention in how cityness is conceived and lived. That this book concludes on this turn should, however, not be seen to imply a teleology; on the contrary, the germs of the hospitable city and of the city as hospice – as much as those of the city of dreams and that of dis-ease – are to be found in the earlier literature, and particularly in that which is informed by the normative philosophy of ubuntu, often glossed as African humanism.[32] *Jozi* implicitly evokes ubuntu when it shows the city in the shape of the hospice; it does so explicitly also in its meditation on the inhospitable city. Senzo, notably, had earlier interrupted a consensus about 'foreigners' in the section titled 'Xenophobia?' with the question: 'what prevents you from treating your brother or sister with hospitality, respect and, yes, even warmth? Have we really moved so far away from the practice of ubuntu?' (Hlongwane 2013: np). (The deliberation takes the form of a 'heated discussion' in a beer and snooker joint that is occasioned by a report in *The Star* newspaper of an actual outbreak of violence in May 2008 that started with the Mozambican national Ernesto Alfabeto Nhumuave being burnt to death in Alexandra.)

The implications of 'ubuntu' (a Nguni word that entered the Oxford English Dictionary in 2018) are often expressed through the proverb '*umuntu ngumuntu ngabantu*' ('a person is a person through other people') – and in which light we should read Frank's earlier introduction to Jozi with the submission that 'a place is its people' (Hlongwane 2014 [2013]: np). The OED quotes Archbishop Desmond Tutu also to the effect that 'ubuntu' names 'our humanness, caring, hospitality, our sense of connectedness, our sense that my humanity is bound up in your humanity'. Nkonko Kamwangamalu's sociolinguistic analysis of the concept reveals further that ubuntu is 'a value according to which the interest of the individual is subordinate to that of the group', and in which 'interdependence', 'communalism' and 'conviviality' is cherished (Kamwangamalu 1999: 27, 24, 25, 29). If the city is typically conceived of as the centre of individual rights, the claim that *Jozi* and others assemble and articulate is one that emphasises instead community, mutuality, responsibility and care. In so doing, they point to the philosophical foundations of the happenstance practices that assemble 'people as infrastructure' (Simone 2008) and through which they find ways of surviving – or, for that matter, of dying with dignity – in the conditions of precarity and ontological insecurity that are endemic to cities of the global south (see Pieterse 2011: 14).[33]

As precarity and the commodification of life are increasingly generalised and globalised in the process that Mbembe (2017 [2013]) describes as 'the becoming black of the world', writing emerging from South Africa today percolates proposals for how cityness might be reclaimed in a context of deepening socio-economic inequality and at a time of climate crisis, mass extinction and global pandemics. It does so by drawing on the imaginative resources of a literature that has long sought to claim forms of cityness in which social life is not dictated by the imperative of extraction, premised on exploitation or withdrawn into exclusive enclaves. Unlike South Africa's dwindling gold reserves, these are renewable resources that may be transferred across generations by new works as well as through re-readings of older ones, and which might also gainfully be exported into the moral and cultural economies of alter-globalisation.

Notes

1 First published in 1960, 'Die Kind' was included in Jonker's collection *Rook en Oker* (1963); the translation delivered in Mandela's address differs slightly from available published versions.

2 The edition used here is translated into South African English; a standard English translation was published by Little, Brown & Co.

3 See Gordin, Tilley, Praksash (2010: 1–2): '[d]espite the name, dystopia is not simply the opposite of utopia [...]; rather, it is a utopia that has gone wrong, or a utopia that functions only for a particular segment of society'; and, '[e]very utopia also comes with its implied dystopia'.

4 That both authors died within months of each other in 2005 while in their early thirties – Mpe from AIDS-related symptoms and Duiker at his own hand – issues sobering commentary on the tenuous nature of this claim.

5 For an argument that the 'corporate city' has its origins in the Dutch East India Company settlement that became Cape Town, see Samuelson (2014a).

6 Pieterse (2011: 9) notes that, across Africa, '[t]he urban poor are the most vulnerable to climate change impacts, and the least able to adapt'.

7 As West-Pavlov (2018b: 149) notes, '[t]he extractive economies treat native labor as a resource on par with the resources to be extracted'.

8 See also Karen Jayes's speculative narrative *For the Mercy of Water* (2013), which is set in a state of water scarcity administered by a multinational subsidiary and given shape by the gendered structures of the extractive colonial-apartheid labour regime: the countryside becomes an extended 'catchment area' while being itself deprived of water; as water is funnelled to the city, young men are driven by thirst to join the forces of 'the company' and the women and girls who remain in the villages are raped and murdered by company guards.

9 Simone (2004: 7) observes that some young urban Africans negotiate their 'disjointed geographies' through recourse to the 'sorceral', which enables them to elaborate a 'counterreality' to that in which 'a discernible future and a life outside of incessant misery have become unthinkable for many'.

10 The line is taken from 'Fragment 2' of what Rampolokeng describes as his 'phefeni note-book' in an interview with Valentine (2013).

11 'Coconut' is a derogatory epithet identifying those who are 'black on the outside and white on the inside'. As Titlestad (2012: 684) notes, '[t]he endless circulation of this metaphor in the post-apartheid public sphere demonstrates that faith in a utopian postracial order has proved naïve'. See Spencer (2009: 68) for

discussion of how Matlwa's novel 'presents a complex articulation of "coconut-tiness"'.

12 For discussion of the trope of 'light' in Wicomb's oeuvre, see Samuelson (2016b: 127–135).

13 Bethlehem (2014: 528) notes that in this dystopia the cellphone functions '[a]s a kind of digital passbook' that 'renders infringement and retribution simultaneous': 'It closes the infinitesimal gap that the passbook left open between the state's interpellation of the racialized body, on the one hand, and the incarceration of the extraction of labour which followed as the consequence of "pass offences", on the other'.

14 'Necropolitics' is Mbembe's advancement on Foucault's concept of 'biopower' and refers to the sovereign 'capacity to dictate who may live and who must die' and 'in which vast populations are subjected to conditions of life conferring upon them the status of the *living dead*' (Mbembe 2003: 11, 40). It has particular pertinence to South Africa under the Mbeki presidency in which people living with HIV/AIDS were denied treatment and 'made to occupy a place between life and death' (Thomas 2014: 151).

15 'Moving around the city', as Bremner (2010: 170) notes of post-apartheid Johannesburg, 'involves constantly negotiating gates, booms, intercom identifications and security checks, transforming life in the city into that of a permanent frontier zone'.

16 Caldeira (2000: 258) describes the 'fortified enclaves' that construct 'private worlds for the elite' in São Paolo as follows: '[t]hey are turned inward, away from the street, whose public life they explicitly reject. They are controlled by armed guards and security systems, which enforce rules of inclusion and exclusion … [T]he enclaves tend to be socially homogenous environments … [and] cultivate a relationship of rupture and denial with the rest of the city and with what can be called a modern style of public space open to free circulation'.

17 Prashad (2012: 14) suggests that such refusals define the global south: '[t]he "global south" has come to refer to this concatenation of protests against the theft of the commons, against the theft of human dignity and rights'; Caldeira (in Gonick 2019) proposes that what cities of the north might thus learn from those of the south are 'political experiments that expand citizenship and affirm rights to the city'.

18 See, inter alia, crime fiction by Andrew Brown, H.J. Golakai, Jassy MacKenzie, Angela Makholwa, Deon Meyer (in Afrikaans), Mike Nicol, Margie Orford, Michele Rowe and Roger Smith.

19 Bauman (2003: 31, 35) notes how flight from the city as a place of assembly manifests as a 'mixophobia' that locates its cure in 'islands of similarity and sameness' which are themselves 'pathogenic' (Bauman 2003: 31, 35).

20 Compare Habermas (1989), who locates deliberative democracy in the public sphere, and Anderson (1983), who argues that the nation as 'imagined community' is produced and sustained by 'print-capitalism'.

21 As Mbembe and Nuttall (2008: 24) observe, 'crime today has become the other side, the underneath, perhaps, of the rise of a culture of consumption'.

22 Kruger (2013: 3) defines Johannesburg as the 'edgy city' in order to highlight 'the historical as well as present conditions of extreme contrasts in plain view'.

23 Compare also Bauman's distinction between 'liquid' and 'heavy' modernity: the latter applies to 'the era of territorial conquest' in which 'wealth and power was

firmly rooted or deposited deep inside the land ... like the beds of iron ore and deposits of coal' (Bauman 2000: 114).

24 For discussion of thrillers set in post-apartheid Cape Town that emplot transnational trafficking rackets, see Samuelson (2014a, 2020).

25 The trope is anticipated in Chris van Wyk's 'About Graffiti' (1979), which imagines graffiti 'wad[ing]' into the city 'unhampered by the tourniquet of influx control'.

26 The international edition published by WW Norton in 2009 instead promises full disclosure with the subtitle 'The City of Johannesburg Unlocked'.

27 Nuttall (2008: 213, 214), who discusses the 'politically charged meaning' of hustling as parodic practice in *Dog Eat Dog*, marks its limits when she notes that it depends on 'turning others into suckers' and implicitly contrasts it to the 'emergent ethic of hospitality in the city' that this chapter turns to in its concluding section.

28 Bauman (2000) and Urry (2014: np) note respectively that 'liquid modernity' is characterised by the dissolving of the bonds that tie individuals into collectives and that the practice of 'offshoring' 'is undermining notions of responsibility'.

29 The phrase 'without /...tenderness / It is hell' is a misquotation from Adrienne Rich's *The Dream of a Common Language*. The contrast I draw between 'tenderness' and 'tenderpreneurs' is somewhat anachronistic as concerns with 'tenderpreneurs' arose some years after Cronin's poem was written; he did, however, became a vocal critic of tender corruption in his role as SACP deputy general secretary.

30 See the 'Xenophobic violence in democratic South Africa timeline' in *South African History Online*: www.sahistory.org.za/article/xenophobic-violence-democratic-south-africa-timeline

31 'If there is a particular ethos of inhabitation that might be identified as predominant across supposedly Southern cities, it entails a relationship of *living-with* – which largely concerns the continuous working out of attention and indifference, reciprocity and individuation, proximity and distance' (Simone 2018: 123).

32 Mphahlele stands out in this respect (see Gaylard 2004), as does Kuzwayo.

33 As Pieterse (2011: 14) notes, attempts to understand such cities are too often clouded by imported theories that 'arise from Northern contexts and assume a well-developed welfare state as an inheritance of Keynesian policies'.

BIBLIOGRAPHY

'About Staffrider' (1978) *Staffrider* 1(1), 1.

Abrahams, Peter (1963 [1946]) *Mine Boy* (Oxford: Heinemann).

Abrahams, Peter (1954) *Tell Freedom* (London: Faber and Faber).

Agamben, Giorgio (2005) *State of Exception*, tr. Attell, K. (Chicago: University of Chicago Press).

Amin, Ash and Thrift, Nigel (2002) *Cities: Reimagining the Urban* (Cambridge: Polity).

Anderson, Benedict (1983) *Imagined Communities: Reflections on the Origin and Spread of Nationalism* (London: Verso).

Attridge, Derek (2012) '"To Speak of This You Would Need the Tongue of a God": On Representing the Trauma of Township Violence', in Mengel, E. and Borzaga, M. (eds.) *Trauma, Memory, and Narrative in the Contemporary South African Novel* (Leiden: Brill), 177–194.

Attwell, David (2005) *Rewriting Modernity: Studies in Black South African Literary History* (Pietermaritzburg: University of KwaZulu-Natal Press).

Attwell, David (2015) *J.M. Coetzee and the Life of Writing* (London: Viking).

Augé, Marc (1995) *Non-Places: Introduction to the Anthropology of Supermodernity*, tr. Howe, J. (London: Verso).

Bakhtin, Mikhail (1981 [1975]) *The Dialogic Imagination: Four Essays*, tr. Emerson, C. and Holquist, M. (Austin: University of Texas Press).

Barnard, Rita (2007) *Apartheid and Beyond: South African Writers and the Politics of Place* (Oxford: Oxford University Press).

Baudelaire, Charles (1964 [1863]) *The Painter of Modern Life and Other Essays*, tr. Mayne, J. (London: Phaidon Press).

Bauman, Zygmunt (2000) *Liquid Modernity* (Cambridge: Polity Press).

Bauman, Zygmunt (2003) *City of Fears, City of Hopes* (London: Goldsmith's College).

Beavon, Keith (2004) *Johannesburg: The Making and Shaping of the City* (Pretoria: Unisa Press).

Berger, Iris (2009) *South Africa in World History* (Oxford: Oxford University Press).

Berlant, Lauren (2011) *Cruel Optimism* (Durham: Duke University Press).

Berman, Marshall (1988) *All That is Solid Melts into Air: The Experience of Modernity* (New York: Penguin).

Bethlehem, Louise (2001) '"A Primary Need as Strong as Hunger": The Rhetoric of Urgency in South African Literary Culture under Apartheid', *Poetics Today* 22(2), 365–389.

Bethlehem, Louise (2014) 'Lauren Beukes's Post-Apartheid Dystopia: Inhabiting *Moxyland*', *Journal of Postcolonial Writing* 50(5), 522–534.

Beukes, Lauren (2008) *Moxyland* (Johannesburg: Jacana).

Beukes, Lauren (2010) *Zoo City* (Johannesburg: Jacana).

Biko, Steve (1987 [1978]) *I Write What I Like: Selected Writings*, ed. Stubbs, C.R. (London: Heinemann).

Blackburn, Douglas (1991 [1908]) *Leaven: A Black and White Story* (Pietermaritzburg: University of Natal Press).

Boehmer, Elleke (1998) 'Endings and New Beginning: Recent South African Fiction', in Attridge, D. and Jolly, R. (eds.) *Writing South Africa: Recent Literature and its Challenges* (Cambridge: Cambridge University Press), 43–56.

Bonner, Philip and Nieftagodien, Noor (2008) *Alexandra: A History* (Johannesburg: Wits University Press).

Bremner, Lindsay J. (2002) 'Closure, Simulation, and "Making Do" in the Contemporary Johannesburg Landscape', in Enwezor, O. et al. (eds.) *Under Siege: Four African Cities—Freetown, Johannesburg, Kinshasa, Lagos* (Ostfildern-Ruit: Hatje Cantz), 153–172.

Bremner, Lindsay (2010) *Writing the City into Being: Essays on Johannesburg, 1998–2008*. (Johannesburg: Fourthwall Books).

Brink, André (2011 [1979]) *A Dry White Season* (London: Vintage Books).

Burgess, Yvonne (1973) *A Life to Live* (Johannesburg: Ad Donker).

Caldeira, Theresa (2000) *City of Walls: Crime, Segregation and Citizenship in São Paulo* (Berkeley: University of California Press).

Castells, Manuel (2010 [1997]) *End of Millennium: Economy, Society and Culture*, vol. 3. Information Age Series, 2nd ed. (Oxford: Wiley-Blackwell).

Castells, Manuel (2004) 'Space of Flows, Space of Places: Materials for a Theory of Urbanism in the Information Age', in Graham, S. (ed.) *The Cybercities Reader* (London: Routledge), 83–93.

Chapman, Michael (1982) 'Introduction', in Chapman, M. (ed.) *Soweto Poetry: Literary Perspectives* (Johannesburg: McGraw-Hill), 11–23.

Chapman, Michael (2001 [1989]) 'More than Telling a Story: *Drum* and Its Significance in Black South African Writing', in Chapman, M. (ed.) *The Drum Decade: Stories from the 1950s* (Pietermaritzburg: University of Natal Press), 183–232.

Clingman, Stephen (1986) *The Novels of Nadine Gordimer: History from the Inside* (London: Allen and Unwin).

Clingman, Stephen (2012) 'Writing in the Interregnum: Literature and the Demise of Apartheid', in Attwell, D. and Attridge, D. (eds.) *Cambridge History of South African Literature* (Cambridge: Cambridge University Press), 633–651.

Coetzee, J.M. (1992 [1974]) 'Man's Fate in the Novels of Alex la Guma', in Attwell, D. (ed.) *Doubling the Point: Essays and Interviews* (Cambridge, MA: Harvard University Press), 344–360.

Coetzee, J.M. (1985 [1983]) *Life & Times of Michael K* (London: Vintage).

Coetzee, J.M. (1988) *White Writing* (New Haven: Yale University Press).

Coetzee, J.M. (1998 [1990]) *Age of Iron* (New York: Penguin).

Comaroff, Jean and Comaroff, John L. (1987) 'The Madman and the Migrant: Work and Labor in the Historical Consciousness of a South African People', *American Ethnologist* 14(2), 191–209.

Comaroff, John L. and Comaroff, Jean (2006) 'Law and Disorder in the Postcolony: An Introduction', in Comaroff, J. and Comaroff, J.L. (eds.) *Law and Disorder in the Postcolony* (Chicago: University of Chicago Press), 1–56.

Comaroff, Jean and Comaroff, John L. (2012) *Theory from the South: Or, How Euro-America is Evolving Toward Africa* (Boulder: Paradigm Books).

Coplan, David B. (1985) *In Township Tonight! South Africa's Black City Music and Theatre* (Johannesburg: Ravan Press).

Coplan, David B. (1994) *In the Time of Cannibals: The Word Music of South Africa's Basotho Migrants* (Chicago: University of Chicago Press).

Couto, Mia (2015) 'Dear President Zuma: A Letter from Mozambican Writer Mia Couto', in Fauvet, P. (tr.) *Daily Maverick*, 20 April. Available at www.dailym averick.co.za/article/2015-04-20-dear-president-zuma-a-letter-from-mozambic an-writer-mia-couto/

Couzens, T. (1985) *The New African: A Study of the Life and Work of H.I.E. Dhlomo* (Johannesburg: Ravan Press).

Crenshaw, Kimberlé (1989) 'Demarginalizing the Intersection of Race and Sex: A Black Feminist Critique of Antidiscrimination Doctrine, Feminist Theory and Antiracist Politics', *University of Chicago Legal Forum*, 139–167.

Cronin, Jeremy (1999 [1997]) 'This City', in *Inside and Out: Poems from Inside and Even the Dead* (Cape Town: David Philip), 118.

Crutzen, Paul J. and Stoermer, Eugene F. (2000) 'The "Anthropocene"', *Global Change Newsletter* 41, 17–18.

Dangarembga, Tsitsi (1988) *Nervous Conditions* (London: The Women's Press).

Dangor, Achmat (1981) *Waiting for Leila* (Johannesburg: Ravan Press).

Dangor, Achmat (1983) *Bulldozer* (Johannesburg: Ravan Press).

Daymond, M.J. et al. (eds.) (2003) *Women Writing Africa: The Southern Region* (New York: Feminist Press).

De Certeau, Michel (1984) *The Practice of Everyday Life*, tr. Rendall, S. (Berkeley, CA: University of California Press).

Derrida, Jacques (2010) 'Hostipitality', tr. Stocker, B. with Morlock, F., *Angelaki* 5(3): 3–18.

Dhlomo, Herbert I.E. (1985 [1941]) 'Valley of a Thousand Hills', in Visser, N. and Couzens, T. (eds.) *H.I.E. Dhlomo: Collected Works* (Johannesburg: Ravan Press), 291–320.

Dhlomo, Herbert I.E. (1985 [1943]) 'The Pass', in Visser, N. and Couzens, T. (eds.) *H.I.E. Dhlomo: Collected Works* (Johannesburg: Ravan Press), 189–210.

Dhlomo, R.R.R. (1928) *An African Tragedy* (Alice: Lovedale Press).

Dlamini, Jacob (2009) *Native Nostalgia* (Johannesburg: Jacana).

Dikobe, Modikwe (1973) *The Marabi Dance* (London: Heinemann).

Dovey, Lindiwe and Impey, Angela (2010) '*African Jim*: Sound, Politics, and Pleasure in Early 'Black' South African Cinema', *Journal of African Cultural Studies* 22(1): 57–73.

Driver, Dorothy (1990) '"M'a-Ngoana O Tsoare Thipa ka Bohaleng – The Child's Mother Grabs the Sharp End of the Knife": Women as Mothers, Women as Writers', in Trump, M. (ed.) *Rendering Things Visible: Essays on South African Literary Culture* (Johannesburg: Ravan Press), 225–255.

Driver, Dorothy (1996) '*Drum* Magazine (1951–9) and the Spatial Configuration of Gender', in Darian-Smith, K., Gunner, L. and Nuttall, S. (eds.) *Text, Theory, Space: Land, Literature and History in South Africa and Australia* (London: Routledge), 231–242.

Driver, Dorothy (2012) 'The Fabulous Fifties: Short Fiction in English', in Atwell, D. and Attridge, D. (eds.) *Cambridge History of South African Literature* (Cambridge: Cambridge University Press), 387–409.

Duiker, K. Sello (2000) *Thirteen Cents* (Cape Town: Kwela Books).

Duiker, K. Sello (2001) *The Quiet Violence of Dreams* (Cape Town: Kwela Books).

Duiker, K. Sello (2004) 'The Streets and the Gods of Truth', *Rhodes Journalism Review* 24, 8–9.

Duiker, K. Sello (2006) *The Hidden Star* (Cape Town: Umuzi Books).

Erlmann, Veit (1991) *African Stars: Studies in Black South African Performance* (Chicago: University of Chicago Press).

Essop, Ahmed (1986 [1967]) *The Hajji & Other Stories* (Johannesburg: Ravan Press).

Fanon, Frantz (1963 [1961]) *The Wretched of the Earth*, tr. Farrington, C. (New York: Grove Press).

Fasselt, Rebecca (2011) 'Ke Nako (it is time) to Scrutinise Ubuntu: Negotiating South African Hospitality towards African Immigrants and Refugees in Patricia Schonstein Pinnock's *Skyline*', in Gallagher, K. (ed.) *Multiculturalism: Critical and Inter-Disciplinary Perspectives* (Oxford: Inter-Disciplinary Press), 177–187.

Fenwick, Mac (1996) '"Tough Guy, eh?" The Gangster-Figure in *Drum*', *Journal of Southern African Studies* 22(4), 617–632.

Fraser, Nancy (1990) 'Rethinking the Public Sphere: A Contribution to the Critique of Actually Existing Democracy', *Social Text* 25/26, 56–80.

Fugard, Athol (1978 [1973]) 'Boesman & Lena', in *Boesman & Lena and Other Plays* (Oxford: Oxford University Press), 237–291.

Fugard, Athol, John Kani and Winston Ntshona (2000 [1972]) 'Sizwe Bansi is Dead', in Walder, D. (ed.) *Athol Fugard: The Township Plays* (Oxford: Oxford University Press), 147–192.

Gasa, Nomboniso (2007) 'Feminisms, Motherisms, Patriarchies and Women's Voices in the 1950s', in Gasa, N. (ed.) *Women in South African History: Basus'iimbokodo, Bawel'imilambo / They Remove Boulders and Cross Rivers* (Cape Town: HSRC Press), 207–229.

Gaylard, Rob (2004) '"Welcome to the World of Our Humanity": (African) Humanism, Ubuntu and Black South African Writing', *Journal of Literary Studies* 20(3–4), 265–282.

Gikandi, Simon (2003) 'Modernity and Modernism', in Gikandi, S. (ed.) *Encyclopedia of African Literature* (London: Routledge), 336–340.

Gonick, Sophie (2019) 'Global Cities and Their Discontents: Saskia Sassen and Teresa Caldeira in Conversation', Public Books, 13 June.

Gordimer, Nadine (1962 [1958]) *A World of Strangers* (London: Penguin).

Gordimer, Nadine (1976 [1968]) 'The Flash of Fireflies', in May, C.E. (ed.) *Short Story Theories* (Athens: Ohio University Press), 178–181.

Gordimer, Nadine (1974) *The Conservationist* (London: Jonathan Cape).

Gordimer, Nadine (1979) *Burger's Daughter* (London: Jonathan Cape).

Gordimer, Nadine (1982 [1981]) *July's People* (London: Penguin Books).

Gordimer, Nadine (1988) 'Living in the Interregnum', in Clingman, S. (ed.) *The Essential Gesture: Writing Politics and Places* (London: Jonathan Cape), 261–284.

Gordimer, Nadine (1998) *The House Gun* (London: Bloomsbury)

Gordimer, Nadine and Ross, Alan (1987) 'Nadine Gordimer: A Writer in South Africa', in Bazin, N. and Seymour, M. (eds.) *Conversations with Nadine Gordimer* (Jacksonville: University Press of Mississippi), 33–42.

Gordin, Michael D., Tilley, Helen and Prakash, Gyan (2010) 'Introduction: Utopia and Dystopia beyond Space and Time', in Gordin, M. et al. (eds.) *Utopia/ Dystopia: Conditions of Historical Possibility* (Princeton: Princeton University Press), 1–17.

Gqola, Pumla Dineo (2001) 'In Search of Female *S/staffriders*: Authority, Gender and Audience, 1978–1982', *Current Writing* 13(2), 31–41.

Gray, Stephen (1985) 'Third World Meets First World: The Theme of "Jim Comes to Joburg" in South African English Fiction", *Kunapipi* 7(2), 61–80.

Gray, Stephen (1991) 'Introduction', in Blackburn, Douglas (ed.) *Leaven: A Black and White Story* (Pietermaritzburg: University of Natal Press), i–xxi.

Gray, Stephen (2006) 'Notes on Sources', in Themba, Can and Gray, S. (ed.) *Requiem for Sophiatown* (London: Penguin), vii–xvi.

Gunner, Liz (2008) 'City Textualities: Isicathamiya, Reciprocities and Voices from the Streets', *Social Dynamics* 34(2), 156–173.

Gwala, M.P. (1973) 'Towards a National Theatre', *South African Outlook*, 132.

Gwala, Mafika (1982 [1979]) 'Black Writing Today', in Chapman, M. (ed.) *Soweto Poetry: Literary Perspectives* (Johannesburg: McGraw-Hill), 169–175.

Gwala, Mafika (1982) *No More Lullabies* (Johannesburg: Ravan Press).

Habermas, Jürgen (1989) *The Structural Transformation of the Public Sphere: An Inquiry into a Category of Bourgeois Society*, tr. Burger, T. with Lawrence, F. (Cambridge, MA: MIT Press).

Harlow, Barbara (1978) *Resistance Literature* (New York: Methuen).

Hart, Deborah M. (1990) 'Political Manipulation of Urban Space: The Razing of District Six', in Jeppie, S. and Soudien, C. (eds.) *The Struggle for District Six: Past and Present* (Cape Town: Buchu Books), 117–142.

Harvey, David (2005) *A Brief History of Neoliberalism* (Oxford: Oxford University Press).

Harvey, David (2012) *Rebel Cities: From the Right to the City to the Urban Revolution* (London: Verso).

Helgesson, Stefan (2006) 'Johannesburg as Africa: A Postcolonial Reading of *The Exploded View* by Ivan Vladislavić', *Scrutiny2*, 11(2), 27–35.

Hlongwane, Perfect (2014 [2013]). *Jozi.* (Johannesburg: Picador Africa Classics).

Hofmeyr, Isabel (1978) 'The Mining Novel in South African Literature: 1870–1920', *English in Africa* 5(2), 1–16.

Hoad, Neville (2006) *African Intimacies: Race, Homosexuality, and Globalization* (Minneapolis: University of Minnesota Press).

Hunter, Eva (1993) 'Zoë Wicomb, Interviewed by Eva Hunter', in Hunter, E. and MacKenzie, C. (eds.) Between the Lines II: Interviews with Nadine Gordimer, Menan du Plessis, Zoë Wicomb, Lauretta Ngcobo (Grahamstown: National English Literary Museum), 79–96.

Jayes, Karen (2013) *For the Mercy of Water* (London: Penguin).

Jones, Megan (2018) 'The Train as Motif in Soweto Poetry', *Journal of Commonwealth Literature* 53(1), 21–42.

Jonker, Ingrid (1963 [1960]) 'Die Kind', in *Rook en Oker* (Johannesburg: Afrikaans Pers-Boekandel), 37.

Joubert, Elsa (1980 [1978]) *The Long Journey of Poppie Nongena* (Johannesburg: Jonathan Ball).

Joubert, Elsa and Meyer, Stephan (2006) 'Creating a Climate for Change', in Coullie, J.L. et al. (eds.) *Selves in Question: Interviews on Southern African Auto/Biography* (Honolulu: University of Hawai'i Press), 173–185.

Kamwangamalu, Nkonko M. (1999) 'Ubuntu in South Africa: A Sociolinguistic Perspective to a Pan-African Concept', *Critical Arts* 13(2), 24–41.

'Kimberley, Northern Cape' (2020) *Wikipedia: The Free Encyclopedia*. Available at https://en.wikipedia.org/wiki/Kimberley,_Northern_Cape

Kirkwood, Mike (1980) 'Staffrider: An Informal Discussion', *English in Africa* 7(2), 22–31.

Kirkwood, Mike (1988) 'Remembering Staffrider', in Oliphant, A. and Vladislavić, I. (eds.) Ten years of Staffrider, 1978–1988 (Johannesburg: Ravan Press), 1–11.

Knecht, Stacy (2005) 'Interview with Ivan Vladislavić', *The Ledge*.

Kossew, Sue (1996) *Pen and Power: A Post-Colonial Reading of J.M. Coetzee and André Brink* (Amsterdam: Rodopi).

Kruger, Loren (2013) *Imagining the Edgy City: Writing, Performing, and Building Johannesburg* (New York: Oxford University Press).

Kuzwayo, Ellen (1985) *Call Me Woman* (London: The Women's Press).

La Guma, Alex (1967 [1962]) *A Walk in the Night and Other Stories* (London: Heinemann).

La Guma, Alex (1988 [1964]) *And a Threefold Cord* (London: Kliptown Books).

Lefebvre, Henri (1996) *Writings on Cities*, tr. and ed. Kofman, E. and Lebas, E. (Oxford: Blackwell).

Le Marcis, Frédéric (2008) 'The Suffering Body of the City', tr. Inggs, J., in Nuttall, S. and Mbembe, A. (eds.) *Johannesburg: The Elusive Metropolis* (Johannesburg: Wits University Press), 170.

Loots, Lliane (1997) 'Re-membering protest theatre in South Africa', *Critical Arts* 11(1–2), 142–152.

Magogodi, Kgafela oa (2004) *Outspoken* (Johannesburg: Laugh-it-Off).

Mahlangu, Songeziwe (2013) *Penumbra* (Cape Town: Kwela Books).

Maimane, Arthur [Arthur Mogale] (2001 [1953]) 'Crime for Sale', in Chapman, M. (ed.) *The Drum Decade: Stories from the 1950s* (Pietermaritzburg: University of Natal Press), 24–31.

Majola, Nja-Mlungu (2002 [1948]) 'To the Land of the Mine Dumps', in Chapman, M. (ed.) *The New Century of South African Poetry* (Johannesburg: Ad Donker), 130.

Mamdani, Mahmood (1996) *Citizen and Subject* (Princeton: Princeton University Press).

Manaka, Matsemela (1981) *Egoli: City of Gold* (Johannesburg: Ravan Press).

Mandela, Nelson (1994a) *Long Walk to Freedom: The Autobiography of Nelson Mandela* (Boston: Little, Brown & Co).

Mandela, Nelson (1994b) 'State of the Nation Address by President of South Africa, Nelson. Mandela, Cape Town', 24 May. Available at www.mandela.gov.za/m andela_speeches/1994/940524_sona.htm

Maponya, Maishe (1981) *The Hungry Earth* (London: Polyptoton).

Marais, Sue (1995) 'Getting Lost in Cape Town: Spatial and Temporal Dislocation in the South African Short Fiction Cycle', *English in Africa* 22(2), 29–43.

Masekela, Hugh (1974) 'Stimela (The Coal Train)', in *I Am Not Afraid* (Audio Recording) (Los Angeles: Wally Heider Studios).

Masilela, Ntongela (2007) *The Cultural Modernity of HIE Dhlomo* (Trenton, NJ: Africa World Press).

Matlou, Joël (1979 [1988]) 'Man Against Himself', in Oliphant, A. and Vladislavić, I. (eds.) *Ten years of Staffrider,1978–1988* (Johannesburg: Ravan Press), 47–57.

Matlou, Joël (1991) *Life at Home and Other Stories* (Johannesburg: COSAW).

Matlwa, Kopana (2007) *Coconut* (Johannesburg: Jacana).

Matshikiza, John (2001) 'Introduction', in Chapman, M. (ed.) *The Drum Decade: Stories from the 1950s* (Pietermartizburg: University of Natal Press), ix–xii.

Matshikiza, John (2008) 'Instant City', in Nuttall, S. and Mbembe, A. (eds.) *Johannesburg: The Elusive Metropolis* (Johannesburg: Wits University Press), 221–238.

Matshikiza, Todd (1961) *Chocolates for My Wife* (London: Hodder & Stoughton).

Matshoba, Mtutuzeli (1979) *Call Me Not a Man: The Stories of Mtutuzeli Matshoba* (Johannesburg: Ravan Press).

Matshoba, Mtutuzeli (1980) 'To Kill a Man's Pride', in Mutloase, Mothobi (ed.) *Forced Landing: Africa South, Contemporary Writings* (Johannesburg: Ravan Press), 103–127.

Mattera, Don (1987) *Memory is the Weapon* (Johannesburg: Ravan Press).

Mbaba, Alfred (2001 [1951]) 'Rhodesia Road', in Chapman, M. (ed.) *The Drum Decade: Stories from the 1950s* (Pietermaritzburg: University of Natal Press), 1–9.

Mbembe, Achille (1992) 'Provisional Notes on the Postcolony', tr. Roitman, J. with Last, M., *Africa* 62(1), 3–377.

Mbembe, Achille (2003) 'Necropolitics', tr. Libby Meintjes, *Public Culture* 15(1), 11–40.

Mbembe, Achille (2008) 'The Aesthetics of Superfluity', in Nuttall, S. and Mbembe, A. (eds.) *Johannesburg: The Elusive Metropolis* (Johannesburg: Wits University Press), 37–67.

Mbembe, Achille and Nuttall, Sarah (2008) 'Introduction: Afropolis', in Nuttall, S. and Mbembe, A. (eds.) *Johannesburg: The Elusive Metropolis* (Johannesburg: Wits University Press), 1–33.

Mbembe, Achille (2017 [2013]) *Critique of Black Reason*, tr. Dubois, L. (Durham: Duke University Press).

Mbembe, Achille (2019) 'Blacks from Elsewhere and the Right of Abode', Ruth First Memorial Lecture 2019, *New Frame*. Available at www.newframe.com/rut h-first-memorial-lecture-2019-achille-mbembe/

McClintock, Anne (1995) *Imperial Leather: Race, Gender and Sexuality in the Colonial Contest* (New York: Routledge).

Mda, Zakes (1995) *Ways of Dying* (Cape Town: Oxford University Press).

Mda, Zakes (2009) *Black Diamonds* (Johannesburg: Penguin Random House).

Meeran, Zinaid (2010) *Saracen at the Gates* (Johannesburg: Jacana).

Meredith, Martin (2007) *Diamonds, Gold, and War* (London: Simon & Schuster).

Mgqwetho, Nontsizi (2007 [1920]) *The Nation's Bounty: The Xhosa Poetry of Nontsizi Mgqwetho*, ed. and tr. Opland, J. (Johannesburg: Wits University Press).

Mhlongo, Niq (2004) *Dog Eat Dog* (Cape Town: Kwela Books).

Mhlongo, Niq (2013) *Way Back Home* (Cape Town: Kwela Books).

Miller, Andie (2011 [2006]) 'Inside the Toolbox: In Conversation with Ivan Vladislavić', in Gaylard, G. (ed.) *Marginal Spaces: Reading Ivan Vladislavić* (Johannesburg: Wits University Press), 211–220.

Modisane, Bloke (2001 [1951]) 'The Dignity of Begging', in Chapman, M. (ed.) *The Drum Decade: Stories from the 1950s* (Pietermaritzburg: University of Natal Press), 10–17.

Modisane, Bloke (1986 [1963]) *Blame Me on History* (Johannesburg: Ad Donker).

Moele, Kgebetli (2007) *Room 207* (Johannesburg: Kwela Books).

Mofokeng, Boitumelo (1989) 'Where are the Women? *Ten Years of Staffrider*', *Current Writing* 1, 41–43.

Moore, Jason W. (2019) 'Who is Responsible for the Climate Crisis?', *Maize*. Available at www.maize.io/en/content/what-is-capitalocene

Morgan, Jonathan & the Great African Spider Writers (2000) *Finding Mr Madini* (Cape Town: David Philip).

Motsisi, Casey (2001 [1958–1959]) 'On the Beat', in Chapman, M. (ed.) *The Drum Decade: Stories from the 1950s* (Pietermaritzburg: University of Natal Press), 175–182.

Moylan, Tom (2000) *Scraps of the Untainted Sky: Science Fiction, Utopia, Dystopia* (Boulder: Westview Press).

Mpe, Phaswane (2001) *Welcome to Our Hillbrow* (Pietermaritzburg: University of Natal Press).

Mpe, Phaswane (2003) '"Our Missing Store of Memories": City, Literature and Representation', in Wasserman, H. and Jacobs, S. (eds.) *Shifting Selves: Post-apartheid Essays on Mass Media, Culture and Identity* (Cape Town: Kwela Books), 181–198.

Mphahlele, Es'kia [Esekie, Bruno] (2001 [1956a]) 'Down the Quiet Street', in Chapman, M. (ed.) *The Drum Decade: Stories from the 1950s* (Pietermaritzburg: University of Natal Press), 94–99.

Mphahlele, Es'kia (2001 [1956b]) 'Lesane' [The Lesanes of Nadia Street] in Chapman, M. (ed.) *The Drum Decade: Stories from the 1950s* (Pietermaritzburg: University of Natal Press), 132–139.

Mphahlele, Es'kia (1959) *Down Second Avenue* (London: Faber & Faber).

Mphahlele, Es'kia (2006 [1967]) 'Mrs Plum', in Mphahlele, Esk'ia (ed.) *In Corner B and Other Stories* (Nairobi: East African Publishing House), 164–208.

Mphahlele, Es'kia (2002 [1973]) 'Exile, the Tyranny of Place and the Literary Compromise', in Ogude, J. et al. (eds.) *Es'kia: Education, African Humanism and Culture, Social Consciousness and Literary Appreciation* (Cape Town: Kwela Books), 277–290.

Mphahlele, Es'kia (1983) 'South African Literature vs the Political Morality (1)', *English Academy Review* 29(1), 14–34.

Mphahlele, Es'kia (1992) 'Landmarks of a Literary History: A Black Perspective', in Chapman, M., Gardner, C. and Mphahlele, E. (eds.) *Perspectives on South African English Literature* (Johannesburg: Ad Donker), 37–59.

Mtshali, Oswald (1971) *Sounds of a Cowhide Drum* (Johannesburg: Renoster).

Mtshali, Oswald (1976) 'Black Poetry in Southern Africa: What It Means', in Heywood, C. (ed.) *Aspects of South African Literature* (London: Heinemann), 121–130.

Mzamane, Mbulelo (1982) *The Children of Soweto* (Johannesburg: Ravan Press).

Mzobe, Sifiso (2010) *Young Blood* (Cape Town: Kwela Books).

Ndebele, Njabulo (1972) 'Black development', in Biko, S. (ed.) *Black Viewpoint* (Durban: Spro-Cas Black Community Programmes), 13–32.

Ndebele, Njabulo (1983) *Fools and Other Stories* (Johannesburg: Ravan Press).

Ndebele, Njabulo (2006 [1991]) *Rediscovery of the Ordinary: Essays on South African Literature and Culture* (Pietermaritzburg: University of KwaZulu-Natal Press).

Ndlovu, Thatshisiwe (2017) 'Fiscal Histories of Sub-Saharan Africa: The Case of South Africa'. *PARI Working Paper Series 2* (Johannesburg: Public Affairs Research Institute).

Ngcobo, Lauretta (1985) 'The African Woman Writer', *Kunapipi* 7(2–3), 81–82.

Ngcobo, Lauretta (1999 [1990]) *And They Didn't Die* (Pietermaritzburg: University of Natal Press).

Ngcobo, Lauretta (1991) 'Women Under Pressure', in Granqvist, R. and Stotesbury, J. (eds.) *African Voices* (Sydney: Dangaroo Press), 48–53.

Nixon, Rob (1994) *Homelands, Harlem, and Hollywood: South African Culture and the World Beyond* (New York: Routledge).

Nkosi, Lewis (2016 [1965]) 'The Fabulous Decade: The Fifties', in Stiebel, L and Chapman, M. (eds.) *Writing Home: Lewis Nkosi on South African Writing* (Pietermaritzburg: University of KwaZulu-Natal Press), 15–48.

Nkosi, Lewis (1972) 'An Obituary on Can Themba', in Themba, Can, Stuart, D. and Hollard, R. (eds.) *The Will to Die* (London: Heinemann), vii–xi.

Nuttall, Sarah (2008) 'Literary City', in Nuttall, S. and Mbembe, A. (eds.) *Johannesburg: The Elusive Metropolis* (Johannesburg: Wits University Press), 195–218.

Nuttall, Sarah and Mbembe, Achille (2015) 'Secrecy's Softwares', *Current Anthropology* 56(12), 317–324.

Ntshanga, Masande (2014) *The Reactive* (Cape Town: Umuzi Books).

Nyamnjoh, Francis B. (2006) *Insiders and Outsiders: Citizenship and Xenophobia in Contemporary Southern Africa* (New York: Zed Books).

Nyamnjoh, Francis B. (2017) 'Incompleteness: Frontier Africa and the Currency of Conviviality', *Journal of Asian and African Studies* 52(3), 253–270.

Nxumalo, Henry [Mr Drum] (2001 [1951]) 'Birth of a Tsotsi', in Chapman, M. (ed.) *The Drum Decade: Stories from the 1950s* (Pietermaritzburg: University of Natal Press), 18–23.

Nxumalo, Henry [Mr Drum] (2001 [1954]) 'Mr Drum goes to Jail', in Chapman, M. (ed.) *The Drum Decade: Stories from the 1950s* (Pietermaritzburg: University of Natal Press), 39–47.

Paton, Alan (2000 [1948]) *Cry, The Beloved Country* (London: Penguin).

Peterson, Bhekizizwe (1990) 'Apartheid and the Political Imagination in Black South African Theatre' *Journal of Southern African Studies* 16(2), 229–245.

Pieterse, Edgar (2011) 'Grasping the Unknowable: Coming to Grips with African Urbanisms' *Social Dynamics* 37(1), 5–23.

Pinnock, Patricia Schonstein (2000) *Skyline* (Cape Town: David Philip).

Plaatje, Solomon Tshekisho (1998 [1916]) *Native Life in South Africa, Before and Since the European War and the Boer Rebellion* (Champaign, IL: Project Gutenberg).

Prashad, Vijay (2012) *The Poorer Nations: A Possible History of the Global South* (London: Verso).

Rabkin, David (1975) 'Drum magazine (1951–1961): And the Works of Black South African Writers Associated with It', Ph.D. thesis. University of Leeds.

Rampolokeng, Lesego (1999) *The Bavino Sermons* (Durban: Gecko Poetry).

Rampolokeng, Lesego (2004) *The H.A.L.F. Ranthology* (Audio recording) (Johannesburg: Mehlo-Maya).

Rive, Richard (1986) *'Buckingham Palace', District Six* (Cape Town: David Philip).

Rive, Richard (1990) 'District Six: Fact and fiction', in Jeppie, S. and Soudien, C. (eds.) *The Struggle for District 6: Past and Present* (Cape Town: Buchu Books), 110–116.

Robinson, Jennifer (2010) 'Living in Dystopia: Past, Present and Future in Contemporary Urban Development', in Prakash, G. (ed.) *Noir Urbanisms: Dystopic Images of the Modern City* (Princeton: Princeton University Press), 218–240.

Rooke, Daphne (1965) *Diamond Jo: A Novel* (London: Victor Gollancz).

Ross, Robert (2008) *A Concise History of South Africa*, 2nd edition (Cambridge: Cambridge University Press).

Roy, Ananya (2009) 'The 21st Century Metropolis: New Geographies of Theory', *Regional Studies* 43(6), 819–830.

Sampson, Anthony (2005 [1956]) *Drum: The Making of a Magazine* (Johannesburg: Jonathan Ball).

Samson, Kathleen (2017) 'From "Sad Black Stories" to "Useful Tragedy": Trajectories of Hope in Johannesburg from Kgebetli Moele's Room 207 to Perfect Hlongwane's Jozi', MA dissertation, University of Cape Town.

Samuelson, Meg (2007) 'The City Beyond the Border: The Urban Worlds of Duiker, Mpe and Vera' *African Identities* 5(2), 247–260.

Samuelson, Meg (2008) 'The Urban Palimpsest: Re-Presenting Sophiatown' *Journal of Postcolonial Writing* 44(1), 63–75.

Samuelson, Meg (2012) 'Writing Women', in Attwell, D. and Attridge, D. (eds.) *Cambridge History of South African Literature* (Cambridge: Cambridge University Press), 757–778.

Samuelson, Meg (2014a) '(Un)Lawful Subjects of Company: Reading Cape Town from Tavern of the Seas to Corporate City', *Interventions: International Journal of Postcolonial Studies* 16(6), 795–817.

Samuelson, Meg (2014b) 'Re-telling Freedom in *Otelo Burning*: The Beach, Surf Noir and *Bildung* at the Lamontville Pool', *Journal of African Cultural Studies* 26(3), 307–327.

Samuelson, Meg (2016a) 'Rendering the Cape-As-Port: Sea-Mountain, Cape of Storms/Good Hope and Adamastor in Local-World Literary Formations', *Journal of Southern African Studies* 42(3), 523–537.

Samuelson, Meg (2016b) 'Reading Nostalgia and Beyond: The Hermeneutics of Suspicion and Race; and, Learning to Read, Again, with Zoë Wicomb', *English in Africa* 43(3), 117–139.

Samuelson, Meg (2020) 'Poaching Plots, Plastic Forms and Ambiguous Goods: Ways of Telling the China-in-Africa Story in the Anthropocene Age', in Rupert, U. and Anthony, R. (eds.) *Reconfiguring Trans-Regionalism in the Global South—African Asian Encounters* (London: Palgrave Macmillan), 97–116.

Sandwith, Corinne (2018) 'Reading and Roaming the Racial City: RRR Dhlomo and *The Bantu World*', *English in Africa* 45(3), 17–39.

Schreiner, Olive (2005 [1899]) 'Words in Season' ['An English-South African's View of the Situation'], *Words in Season: The Public Writings with Her Own Remembrances Collected for the First Time*, ed. Gray, S. (London: Penguin), 59–101.

Schreiner, Olive (1923) *Thoughts on South Africa*, ed. Cronwright-Schreiner, S.C. (London: T Fisher Unwin).

Schreiner, Olive ([1974] c1873) 'Diamond Fields: Only a Story of Course', ed. Rive, R., *English in Africa* 1(1), 15–29.

Segooa, Demetrius (1982 [1941]) 'Praises of the Train (*Translated from the Sotho*)', in Chapman, M. and Dangor, A. (eds.) *Voices from Within: Black Poetry from South Africa* (Johannesburg: Ad Donker), 62–63.

Sepamla, Sipho (1975) *Hurry Up To It!* (Johannesburg: Ad Donker).

Sepamla, Sipho (1980) 'The Thrust of Black Writing Since the Mid-Sixties: A Subjective View' in Mphahelele, E. and Couzens, T. (eds.) *The Voice of the Black Writer in Africa* (Johannesburg: University of the Witwatersrand Press), 25.

Sepamla, Sipho (1981) *A Ride on the Whirlwind* (Johannesburg: Ad Donker).

Serote, Mongane Wally (1983 [1972]) *Yakhal'inkomo* (Johannesburg: Ad Donker).

Serote, Mongane Wally (1975) *No Baby Must Weep* (Johannesburg: Ad Donker).

Serote, Mongane Wally (1978) *Behold Mama, Flowers* (Johannesburg: Ad Donker).

Serote, Mongane Wally (1981) *To Every Birth its Blood* (Johannesburg: Ravan Press).

Sheller, Mimi and John Urry (2004) 'The City and the Car', in Miles, M. et al. (eds.) *The Cities Culture Reader* (New York: Routledge), 202–218.

Sheringham, Michael (1996) 'City Space, Mental Space, Poetic Space: Paris in Breton, Benjamin and Réda', in Sheringham, M. (ed.) *Parisian Fields* (London: Reaktion Books), 85–114.

Simmel, Georg (2004 [1903]) 'The Metropolis and Mental Life', tr. Wolff, K. (1950) in Miles, M. et al. (eds.) *The Cities Culture Reader* (New York: Routledge), 12–19.

Simone, AbdouMaliq (2004) *For the City Yet to Come: Changing African Life in Four Cities* (Durham: Duke University Press).

Simone, AbdouMaliq (2008) 'People as Infrastructure', in Nuttall, S. and Mbembe, A. (eds.) *Johannesburg: The Elusive Metropolis* (Johannesburg: Wits University Press), 221–238.

Simone, AbdouMaliq (2018) 'Inoperable Relations and Urban Change in the Global South', in West-Pavlov, R. (ed.) *The Global South and Literature* (Cambridge: Cambridge University Press), 123–133.

Soja, Edward W. (1997) 'Six Discourses on the Postmetropolis', in Westwood, S. and Williams, J. (eds.) *Imagining Cities: Scripts, Signs, Memories* (London: Routledge), 19–30.

Sole, Kelwyn (2010) 'Cape Town™', *New Contrast*.

Spencer, Lynda (2009) 'Young, black and female in post-apartheid South Africa: Identity Politics in Kopana Matlwa's *Coconut*', *Scrutiny2* 14(1), 66–78.

Swanson, Donald (dir.) (1949) *African Jim, aka Jim Comes to Jo'burg* (Feature film) (Johannesburg: Warrior Films).

Themba, Can (1985 [1953]) 'Mob Passion', in Patel, E. (ed.) *The World of Can Themba* (Johannesburg: Ravan Press), 9–20.

Themba, Can (2001 [1955]) 'Baby Come Duze', in Chapman, M. (ed.) *The Drum Decade: Stories from the 1950s* (Pietermaritzburg: University of Natal Press), 109–114.

Themba, Can (1985 [1957]) 'The Life and Love of Dolly Rathebe', in Patel, E. (ed.) *The World of Can Themba* (Johannesburg: Ravan Press), 175–205.

Themba, Can (1972 [1957]) 'Terror on the Trains', in Stuart, D. and Holland, R. (eds.) *The Will to Die* (London: Heinemann), 68–71.

Themba, Can (1972 [1959]) 'Requiem for Sophiatown', in Stuart, D. and Holland, R. (eds.) *The Will to Die* (London: Heinemann), 102–107.

Themba, Can (1972 [1961]) 'Bottom of the Bottle', in Stuart, D. and Holland, R. (eds.) *The Will to Die* (London: Heinemann), 108–115.

Themba, Can (1972 [1964]) 'Dube Train', in Stuart, D. and Holland, R. (eds.) *The Will to Die* (London: Heinemann), 57–62.

Themba, Can (1972a) 'Crepuscule', in Stuart, D. and Holland, R. (eds.) *The Will to Die* (London: Heinemann), 2–13.

Themba, Can (1972b) 'The Will To Die', in Stuart, D. and Holland, R. (eds.) *The Will to Die* (London: Heinemann), 62–66.

Thomas, Kylie (2014) *Impossible Mourning: HIV/AIDS and Visuality After Apartheid* (Johannesburg: Wits University Press).

Titlestad, Michael (2004) *Making the Change: Jazz in South African Literature and Reportage* (Pretoria: Unisa Press).

Titlestad, Michael (2012) 'Writing the City After Apartheid', in Attwell, D. and Attridge, D. (eds.) *Cambridge History of South African Literature* (Cambridge: Cambridge University Press), 676–694.

Tlali, Miriam (1979) *Muriel at Metropolitan* (London: Longman).

Tlali, Miriam (1980) *Amandla* (Johannesburg: Ravan Press).

Tlali, Miriam (1989) *Footprints in the Quag: Stories and Dialogues from Soweto* (Cape Town: David Philip).

'Ubuntu' (2018) *Oxford English Dictionary* (Oxford: Oxford University Press).

Urry, John (2014) *Offshoring* (Cambridge: Polity Press).

Valentine, Douglas (2013) 'Post-Freedom Poetry' [Interview with Lesego Rampolokeng], *Counterpunch*, 13 September. Available at www.counterpunch .org/2013/09/13/post-freedom-poetry//

Van der Merwe, Annari (2005) 'Tribute' in Mzamane, M. Z. (ed.) *Words Gone Two Soon: A Tribute to Phaswane Mpe and K. Sello Duiker* (Pretoria: Umgangatho), 5–14.

Van Niekerk, Marlene (1999 [1994]) *Triomf*, tr. De Kock, L. (Johannesburg: Jonathan Ball).

Van Wyk, Chris (1979) 'About Graffiti', in *It Is Time to Go Home* (Johannesburg: Ad Donker), 13–15.

Van Wyk, Chris and Oliphant, Andries (1988) 'Interview with Chris Van Wyk', in Oliphant, A. and Valdislavic, I. (eds.) *Ten Years of Staffrider, 1978–1988* (Johannesburg: Ravan Press), 165–172.

Van Wyk, Chris (2004) *Shirley, Mercy and Goodness: A Childhood Memoir* (Johannesburg: Picador).

Vaughn, Michael (1982) 'Literature and Politics: Currents in South African Writing in the Seventies', *Journal of Southern African Studies* 9(1), 118–138.

Vilakazi, B.W. (1973 [1945]) *Zulu Horizons*, tr. Malcolm, D.M. and Friedman, F.L. (Johannesburg: University of Witwatersrand Press).

Visser, Nick (1987) 'Fictional Projects and the Irruptions of History: Mongane Serote's *To Every Birth Its Blood*', *English Academy Review* 4(1), 67–76.

Vladislavić, Ivan (2001) *The Restless Supermarket* (Cape Town: David Philip).

Vladislavić, Ivan (2004) *The Exploded View* (Johannesburg: Penguin Random House).

Vladislavić, Ivan (2006a) *Portrait with Keys* (Cape Town: Umuzi).

Vladislavić, Ivan (2006b) 'X Marks the Spot', *Scrutiny2* 11(2), 125–128.

Vladislavić, Ivan (2008) 'Staffrider', *Chimurenga*, March. Available at http://chi murengalibrary.co.za/staffrider-an-essay-by-ivan-vladislavic

Vladislavić, Ivan (2011) *Double Negative* (Cape Town: Umuzi).

Wade, Michael (1994) 'Trains as Tropes: The Role of the Railway in Some South African Literary Texts', in Boehmer, E., Chrisman, L. and Parker, K. (eds.) *Altered State? Writing and South Africa* (Sydney: Dangaroo), 75–90.

Wark, McKenzie (2011) *The Beach Beneath the Street: The Everyday Life and Glorious Times of the Situationist International* (London: Verso).

Warner, Michael (2002) *Publics and Counterpublics* (New York: Zone Books).

Watson, Stephen (1986) *In This City: Poems* (Cape Town: David Philip).

West-Pavlov, Russell (2018a) 'Toward the Global South: Concept of Chimera, Paradigm of Panacea?', in West-Pavlov, R. (ed.) *The Global South and Literature* (Cambridge: Cambridge University Press), 1–19.

West-Pavlov, Russell (2018b) 'Extractive Industries in the Global South: Development, Necropolitics, Globalization, and Planetary Ethics', in West-Pavlov, R. (ed.) *The Global South and Literature* (Cambridge: Cambridge University Press), 145–160.

Wicomb, Zoë (1987) *You Can't Get Lost in Cape Town* (London: Virago).

Wicomb, Zoë (2018 [1990]) 'To Hear the Variety of Discourses', in Van der Vlies, A. (ed.) *Race, Nation, Translation: South African Essays, 1990–2013* (Yale: Yale University Press), 81–91.

Wicomb, Zoë (2006) *Playing in the Light* (Cape Town: Umuzi).

Wilkinson, Jane (1990) 'Serote's Cities: (de-)Constructing South African Urban Space', *Africa* 45(3), 485–493.

Williams, Raymond (1975) *The Country and the City* (St Albans: Paladin).

Williams, Raymond (1977) 'Structures of Feeling', in *Marxism and Literature, Part II: Cultural Theory* (Oxford: Oxford University Press), 128–135.

Zondi, N. (2011) 'Three Protagonists in B.W. Vilakazi's "Ezinkomponi" ("On the Mine Compounds")', *Literator* 32(2), 173–187.

INDEX

Note: Page numbers followed by 'n' refer to notes. Literary works are found under the authors' names as well as separately.